Bradfc

TROLLEYBUSES

Stephen Lockwood
Series editor Robert J Harley

MP Middleton Press

Cover Photograph: Depicted here is the final development of the Bradford Trolleybus, a modern, front entrance double decker, which compared very favourably with the motorbuses of the time. One of the very first of this type was Karrier 792, originally a single decker from Darlington in County Durham, which entered service in Bradford with this new East Lancs body in December 1958. It is seen pausing to pick up a passenger during the climb to Allerton. The very generous level of passenger comfort offered by these vehicles, with platform doors and heaters, was meant to attract and retain passengers. Therefore, it seems perverse that such a trolleybus had advertising for Austin cars along its side.
(Photobus/J.Copland)

*Back Cover text: This is based on **60 Years of Trolleybuses** booklet issued by Bradford City Transport in 1961.*

Published November 2003

ISBN 1 904474 19 5

© Middleton Press, 2003

| *Design* | *Deborah Esher* |
| | *David Pede* |

Published by
> *Middleton Press*
> *Easebourne Lane*
> *Midhurst, West Sussex*
> *GU29 9AZ*

Tel: 01730 813169
Fax: 01730 812601
Email: info@middletonpress.co.uk
www.middletonpress.co.uk

Printed & bound by MPG Books, Bodmin, Cornwall

CONTENTS

1	The Railless Years	1	11	Crossflatts	49
2	Bankfoot to Bolton	6	12	Bradford Moor	56
3	Clayton	15	13	Thornbury	60
4	Allerton	21	14	Wibsey and Buttershaw	62
5	Saltaire via Thackley	24	15	St. Enoch's Road Top	64
6	Greengates	28	16	Around the City Centre	69
7	Eccleshill	30	17	Driver Training	88
8	Thornton	35	18	Depots and Works	90
9	Duckworth Lane	39	19	Rolling Stock	95
10	Tong Cemetery and Holme Wood	46	20	Finale	118

INTRODUCTION AND ACKNOWLEDGEMENTS

The First, the Last and the Greatest! This is Bradford's place in British trolleybus history. However, as a native of nearby Huddersfield, I could never wholly subscribe to the last of these claims and I suspect that Londoners, Wulfrunians and those from other well known former trolleybus towns would also make a similar case against giving Bradford the top accolade. Nevertheless, whatever anyone's allegiances, there is no doubt that the Bradford system, through its history, development and sheer longevity was one of those at the 'top of the tree'.

In my younger days I lived close to Bradford Road in Huddersfield and it was just over a thirty minute bus ride into Bradford, the nearest big city. My father was an inveterate book collector (of all subjects) and he would often take me there on shopping expeditions. On the descent from Odsal Top into Bradford there would be a fleeting glimpse of the terminal loop of the trolleybus service 34 at Bankfoot together with a blue and cream trolleybus, invariably, it seemed, with an advert for 'Lanry' across its rear. In the city centre there were trolleybuses everywhere, all four wheelers (a novelty for me), nipping about around every visible street corner. Each service seemed to have its own pair of wires, and, as an expert on car numbers (as most boys of that age were) many of the trolleybuses had registration letters that were completely strange and definitely not the familiar Bradford marks. One other impression was that there was no doubt at all where trolleybuses heading for the central area were going – the message was bold and clear with typical Yorkshire bluntness – 'CITY'. With luck we would lunch at Collinson's

Café in Tyrrel Street where from the upstairs restaurant I could see the trolley-heads passing by every few seconds.

Later excursions involved accompanying my mother to visit elderly relatives at Bradford Royal Infirmary and this involved trolleybus rides on the famous service 8 to Duckworth Lane. The constant stream of vehicles on this route meant never having to wait more than a minute or two – and what vehicles they were. These were trolleybuses with front entrances and power operated doors just like the latest motorbuses on the Huddersfield route. They didn't, of course, grind and crawl up the hills like motorbuses, but swept up the gradients of Sunbridge Road and Whetley Hill without any obvious effort at all.

My most intimate experiences with Bradford's trolleybuses came when I left school in 1967. In those days jobs were reasonably plentiful and I accepted an opportunity to become a clerical officer with Bradford City Transport at its Forster Square head office. Starting in the Purchasing Department, I remember for instance, processing orders for 'grooved cadmium copper trolley wire'. A move to the Traffic Office involved me allocating drivers and conductors to crew workings, including, I recall, the crew of the last ever trolleybus to Clayton. Just prior to the final trolleybus closure I was working in the Schedules Office learning the art of timetable compilation. Needless to say, I made sure that I was given the job of writing out all the vehicle running boards concerned with the final trolleybus closure (including those of the last service trolleybuses and the ceremonial last vehicle).

Working in Bradford enabled me to explore the system in my lunch hour. Regular trips to

Duckworth Lane, St Enoch's Road Top and Five Lane Ends could comfortably be made within an hour. At this time, in the last four years of the system, there were still 90 trolleybuses in service of which three were the last of AEC make still running. Even by mid 1971, when Bradford was the only trolleybus operator left, there was still a sizeable system of 51 vehicles operating over five main routes and seven termini.

This book is a photographic journey around the City's trolleybus routes to give readers a taste of what the system was like, and bring back memories. It is not meant to be a fully detailed history of the system. For this, readers are directed to the books by Stanley King and John Stainforth/ Harold Brearley, whose works have been consulted for this volume. I have arranged our tour, route by route, in the date order that each service was introduced, then following with a section showing trolleybuses in the city centre. The selection of photographs has been very difficult due to having to show as many facets as possible of this large system in 120 views. I have tried to select views that have not been previously seen. My thanks go to the many photographers who have so willingly given permission to reproduce their work here and to those unknown contributors who it has proved impossible to identify.

The text has been read by the following three valued colleagues who have suggested improvements and additions where they saw fit.

Firstly, that elder statesman of Bradford Transport, Stanley King, who in the latter years of the system was Deputy Convenor of the Transport Executive Group of Bradford City Council and did much to promote the advantages of the trolleybus in the city. He is still a member of Bradford Metropolitan Council and continues to encourage the Council to consider the trolleybus in future transport strategies. Stanley's trilogy on Bradford's transport history (Venture Publications) was published during the 1990s and all readers are recommended to read this work. He also very kindly allowed me the pick of his vast collection of Bradford trolleybus photographs for use herein. Secondly, to my friend and fellow author Peter Cardno of Stockton and finally to Philip Jenkinson of Huddersfield, whose constructive criticism of my syntax is very much appreciated.

The overhead wiring maps are based on those that originally appeared in the John Stainforth/Harold Brearley book 'The Bradford Trolleybus System' published in 1971 and I am grateful for permission to adapt these.

Thanks are also due to my publisher Vic Mitchell who suggested this work and to Roy Brook, David Smithies, David Beach and Paul Watson, who have all provided specific assistance.

Finally I wish to pay tribute to the patience and unfailing encouragement of my wife Eileen, as well as to her very useful proof reading skills.

GEOGRAPHICAL SETTING

Bradford is a city in the Metropolitan County of West Yorkshire and during the 1950s and 1960s had a population of 298,000. The city is famous for wool and textile processing - one of the most important extant Victorian buildings in the city centre being the Wool Exchange built in 1867. Nearby large settlements, all situated about 10 miles away, are Leeds to the east, (Bradford's larger rival city that Bradfordians sometimes mockingly refer to as 'that other place'); Huddersfield to the south; Halifax to the west; and Keighley to the north-west.

The city itself is situated in a natural bowl and therefore almost all roads out of it involve a steep climb. This feature alone made Bradford ideal for trolleybus operation. Two of the steepest climbs were Church Bank beside the Cathedral on the Bradford Moor route (1 in 9.8) and Whetley Hill on the Duckworth Lane service (1 in 9.7).

Administratively, Bradford became a County Borough in 1889 and achieved City status in 1897. It is now part of an enlarged Bradford Metropolitan District created in 1974. The Town Hall, which figured as a background to many trolleybus photographs, was opened in 1873 and re-named City Hall in 1965. Its famous carillon played a part in the closing ceremony of the trolleybus system as we shall see.

HISTORICAL BACKGROUND

Trolleybus operation in Bradford spread over 60 years. The 'railless' service (as the trolleybus was then known) opened on 20th June 1911, the year Bradford City won the F.A Cup, and closed on 26th March 1972, the year after decimal coinage was introduced.

Editor's Note: In the early years of trolleybus operation in Britain a number of words were used to describe the vehicles, which to contemporary eyes resembled tramcars not tied to a fixed set of rails. Terms such as railless cars, trackless cars, trolley omnibuses and trolley vehicles were all current during the first three decades of the twentieth century. Ironically, although this form of transport has died out in the UK, the English word 'trolleybus' now exists in many languages across the globe.

In 1898, only thirteen years before the advent of the railless, Bradford Corporation had opened its first electric tramway between Forster Square and Bolton Junction via Bolton Road. By 1903 the Corporation electric trams had replaced the steam and horse trams previously operated by private companies. The system developed up to 1914 when the last extension was opened between Bingley and Crossflatts. Because of the narrow track gauge (4ft/1219mm), and the exposed nature of some routes, the Board of Trade would not allow the cars to be fully enclosed. Through running with the neighbouring tramway system of Leeds, which used standard gauge, was achieved as a result of the innovative thinking of the Bradford Tramways manager, CJ Spencer. He devised a tram truck with adjustable wheel-sets and this, combined with a length of tapering track at the Bradford/Leeds boundary at Stanningley, enabled Bradford and Leeds trams to work a through service between the two cities during the period 1909 to 1918.

The Bradford manager was considering innovation of a different kind in 1909. He desired to introduce services on routes with low traffic potential that would feed into the tram network. Together with managers from Leeds and Sheffield, Mr Spencer undertook a visit to fledgling trolleybus systems operating in Berlin, Vienna and Milan as well as inspecting a railless vehicle being demonstrated in Hendon, London. The result was that Bradford, obtained powers to operate a railless trolleybus service along Sticker Lane,

between Dudley Hill and Laisterdyke, connecting two tramway corridors. Two railless vehicles were obtained with tram-like Hurst Nelson single deck bodies and the service was officially opened on 20th June 1911, carefully timed to coincide with the opening of a similar service in Leeds. Public service began on 24th June. Known as the 'Penny Joss' due to the uneven state of the roadway, the railless was deemed a success and in 1914 the service was extended at both ends. On 17th July the service opened along Rooley Lane from Dudley Hill to Bankfoot, connecting with the Manchester Road trams. Beyond Laisterdyke, an extension via Killinghall Road to Bolton Junction opened on 13th October, connecting with the Bolton trams and crossing en route the Bradford Moor and Undercliffe tram routes.

In the meantime another separate railless route had been introduced on 25th June 1914 from the tramway at Odsal Top to Oakenshaw. The initial wiring on this section was basic, with only a single set of wires provided for the one vehicle shuttle. By 1922 normal two way wiring had been provided. These extensions resulted in a further 18 railless vehicles being put into service, these being assembled at the Corporation's own workshops at Thornbury. The first of these was tested on an isolated length of wiring in Queens Road, between Manningham Lane and Manningham Station, which was never used for passenger service, although it survived until 1926.

The next development was the introduction of a service running from the city centre and not feeding into a tram service. This ran from Forster Square along Canal Road to Frizinghall, with inward journeys diverting via Bolton Woods. This awkward arrangement was simplified in 1918 when the service was run as two separate routes turning via a loop at Frizinghall and a reverser at Bolton Woods. The former connecting wires along Gaisby Lane were henceforth abandoned.

More innovation occurred during the First World War when the two original railless cars were converted into trolley-lorries carrying goods and parcels to local mills and even operating through to Leeds. This was made possible by using a skate in the tram tracks to complete the electrical traction circuit. Two covered top double deck railless vehicles, the first in the world, entered service in 1920 and 1922 respectively. The second of these was a six wheeler with two axles at the front and both were unlikely looking contraptions and known as 'flying cottage loaves'.

Another new route opened in 1926 from Town Hall Square to Clayton, which at that time was outside the Bradford boundary. This service did not feed a tramway route, but duplicated the Lidget Green trams for the first 1½ miles out from the city centre. The Oakenshaw route was extended down Manchester Road into the city centre the following year, again parallel to the trams. In 1928 a through service was started between Oakenshaw and Clayton via Town Hall Square.

The success of the railless led, in 1929, to the decision to replace tram routes with trolleybuses. On 1st December 1929, trolleybuses took over the Allerton tram service using double deck six wheel vehicles. The Saltaire via Thackley trams were similarly replaced on 30th March 1930, followed by the branch to Idle and Greengates on 22nd March 1931. On the debit side, the poorly patronised Frizinghall/Bolton Woods services were abandoned altogether on 30th April 1932. This was part of a deal with West Yorkshire Road Car Co, who agreed to discontinue their competing buses on the Clayton service. The Lidget Green trams were incorporated into the Clayton trolleybus service in December 1934.

Throughout the rest of the 1930s tram routes were steadily converted to trolleybus operation, apart from the Heaton and Undercliffe services which went over to motorbuses in 1935. The dates of these conversions were :-

Eccleshill	30th May 1934
Thornton	21st November 1934
Duckworth Lane	2nd October 1935 (extended to the Infirmary 1936)
Tong Cemetery	6th July 1938
Crossflatts	7th May 1939

For the Thornton conversion and onwards, 'modern' trolleybuses with motorbus, rather than tram, features were used. Also, for the first time, trolleybuses were able to show route numbers. These had been used previously in timetables, and now, following a revision of the allocation of numbers to routes, they were shown on the vehicles. Firmly believing in the principle of supporting home industries, the Corporation consistently purchased electrical equipment made by English Electric at their Bradford Moor factory as well as AEC chassis built at Southall, Middlesex.

Wartime conditions brought about the closure of the Oakenshaw railless on 1st August 1940. Interestingly the wiring between Odsal Top and the city centre was retained and used by the Manchester Road trams until 1950.

The war also resulted in significant vehicle developments. Large numbers of wartime Sunbeam and Karrier utility trolleybuses entered service between 1942 and 1946, the first 10 being a diverted order from Johannesburg with eight feet wide bodies. Nine of the 1934 AEC trolleybuses were given new Brush utility style bodies and started a process of rebodying older chassis that continued for the next twenty years. Also, Southend Corporation loaned four AEC trolleybuses (nos 124 to 127) for a period, operating from Saltaire depot. Their light blue livery had a lasting effect on Bradford's own colours, and a similar light blue was adopted for the home fleet shortly afterwards.

The closing of tram routes continued during and after the war, but these were replaced by motorbus services because of the difficulties of obtaining new trolleybuses in this period. However plans were made to introduce trolleybuses on the Bradford Moor and Undercliffe services. (The Undercliffe trams, converted to buses in 1935, had returned to the route in 1939). Accordingly, orders were placed for the first post-war trolleybuses, resulting in 20 BUT type vehicles, 8 feet wide, being delivered between 1949 and 1951. The Bradford Moor route became trolleybus operated on 4th December 1949, and on the first day of the new decade it was extended as a through service with the Crossflatts route, as the former trams had been. The Undercliffe route never got its trolleybuses, and their future in Bradford at this point, shortly after the nationalisation of the electricity industry which ended the supply of cheap municipally generated power, was far from secure.

One of the most significant developments in Bradford's trolleybus history occurred during 1951–the appointment of Chaceley Humpidge as General Manager. He immediately realised their potential and set about completely revitalising the system. From 2nd March 1952, the Thornbury motorbus service (no 89), along the entire length of which there was already trolleybus wiring for depot access purposes, went over to trolleybuses. Plans were made for the expansion of the system including the replacement of motorbus services and a long overdue cross-city connection between Forster Square and Town Hall Square via Broadway. This link was completed in June 1954, but difficulties in terminating trolleybuses in the Victoria Square area put the plan on hold.

Extensions to the system followed throughout the decade. The Wibsey motorbus route became trolleybus operated from 24th April 1955 and a branch off this to the Buttershaw housing estate followed on 8th April 1956. The cross–city service via Broadway eventually opened on 3rd November 1957, running through from Eccleshill to St Enoch's Road Top on the Wibsey route. Further expansion was introduced as follows:

Clayton (Black Bull) to Clayton (The Avenue)
15th July 1956
Eccleshill (Mechanics Institute to Faltis Square)
9th August 1959
Holme Wood (a branch off the Tong Cemetery route)
6th March 1960

In addition, a new service from the city centre to Bierley Church was introduced during the Suez crisis of 1956/7, for which very little new wiring was required.

Additional vehicles to support this expansion came via the judicious purchase of second-hand trolleybuses, which were being discarded, often prematurely, by other operators. The whole operational fleets of Notts and Derby Traction Co and Darlington Corporation were acquired. Other additions came from Llanelly, St Helens, Brighton, and Hastings. From January 1956, both existing pre-war and wartime vehicles, and some of the second hand purchases, began to enter service with new East Lancashire Coachbuilders bodies of modern design, some with platform doors. This design was developed as the rebodying programme progressed and the former Darlington trolleybuses, together with many of Bradford's wartime utility vehicles, were given front entrance bodies and some even had experimental trolley retriever gear.

In June 1961, Bradford celebrated 50 years of trolleybus operation by the painting of two pre-war vehicles in old liveries. This Jubilee year celebration turned out to be the climax of the system's history. The network was run with 193 vehicles, many of them with modern bodies. The wiring was well maintained and used modern methods of construction with curved segments and interlaced frogs, which saved space and weight. Wiring provision was generous, especially in the city centre, where duplicate wires and passing loops prevented trolleybuses being delayed by each other. Most of the termini had turning circles at wide road junctions or in purpose built lay-bys. The triangular reverser, common on other systems, was never widely used in Bradford, although the lack of space for a turning circle forced such a device to be used on the last trolleybus extension in Holme Wood estate.

The following year, Mr Humpidge left to further his career and his replacement immediately placed orders for a large batch of AEC motorbuses. The tide was turning against the Bradford trolleybus. Massive redevelopment works in the city centre would require considerable diversion to trolleybus services and it was evident that the most affected ones were to be replaced by motorbuses. Accordingly, on 17th November 1962, the Bradford Moor service and the through route from Eccleshill to St Enoch's Road Top were closed in advance of the Forster Square redevelopment. Another change of General Manager occurred in 1963, when Edward Deakin took the reins. He was an avuncular figure and, whilst he was sympathetic to the trolleybus system, it was evident that there would not be any further development, though the existing vehicles and infrastructure would be maintained as long as economically possible. The long Crossflatts route, which, since the loss of the Bradford Moor service a year earlier, had terminated at a temporary turning circle at the bottom of Cheapside, closed on 31st October 1963 in the face of further city centre development. Despite these contractions, the last of the rebodied second hand vehicles entered service in 1962/3, these being twelve BUT and Sunbeam vehicles from Doncaster and Mexborough. These really were fine trolleybuses and compared very favourably with the lightweight bodied motorbuses, with noisy diesel engines, which entered service at the same time.

The remainder of the decade and up to the beginning of 1971 saw further trolleybus route losses. All these were as a result of general bus service reorganisations or, in the case of the Wakefield Road routes, because of major road reconstruction. Closure dates were:

Bolton-Bankfoot	29th February 1964
Eccleshill	31st October 1964
Tong Cemetery/Holme Wood	1st April 1967
Clayton (The Avenue to The 'Black Bull')	30th May 1970
Allerton	27th February 1971

In the meantime, redevelopment of the Town Hall Square area resulted in the Wibsey and Buttershaw trolleybuses being diverted onto a new road alongside the Gaumont cinema known as Princes Way. The new outward bound wiring here, brought into use on 21st September 1969, was the last such new installation on a public road in Britain.

By April 1971, with the closure of the Teesside trolleybus system, Bradford had become the last operator of such vehicles in Britain and the system celebrated its 60th (Golden Jubilee) anniversary in June. The economics of continuing operation, over what was no longer a co-ordinated network, were seen to be untenable and orders had been placed for sufficient motorbuses to replace the 51 trolleybuses left in service. On 30th June 1971 the Bolton Road routes to Saltaire and Greengates ran for the last time, followed a month later on 31st July by the Clayton and Wibsey/Buttershaw routes. This left two services, both operating out of Duckworth Lane depot, (Thornton to Thornbury, and Duckworth Lane). On 8th November 1971 this last bastion of trolleybuses was invaded when motorbuses began to operate some duties on the Duckworth Lane route. This effectively reduced trolleybuses on this service to peak hour operation, but the Thornton to Thornbury section usually retained a full trolleybus allocation.

Events now took an unexpected turn. A strike by coal industry workers in early 1972 resulted in power cuts and the trolleybus service was withdrawn entirely after operation on 10th February. Against all odds, the situation had improved by the following month, and on 7th March, 11 trolleybuses returned to Duckworth Lane Depot to resume part operation of the two services. Plans were laid to commemorate the closing of the system, the date of which was set for Friday 24th March. Accordingly, the last public service trolleybuses operated on this date. The following day, and on Sunday morning 26th March, pre-bookable tours of the system were operated, followed by the ceremonial last run at 3pm. Bradford and Britain's last official trolleybus, no 844, was suitably inscribed and it arrived at Thornbury depot just before 4.30pm. For Bradford and Britain, the trolleybus era had ended.

Bradford Trolleybus Route numbers as at June 1961

5	Bell Dean Road*
6	Spring Head Road*
7	Thornton
	(extended across City to Thornbury in 1965)
8	Duckworth Lane
16	Bierley Church*
17	Holme Wood
18	Tong Cemetery
19	Dudley Hill*
24	Crossflatts
25	Saltaire*
26	Bingley*
27	Frizinghall*-City-Chelmsford Road*
30	Bradford Moor
31	Allerton (re-numbered 16 in 1966)
32	Chapel Lane*
33	Eccleshill
34	Bolton - Bankfoot
37	Clayton
38	Pasture Lane*
39	Lidget Green*
40	Saltaire via Thackley
41	Thackley*
42	Greengates
43	Five Lane Ends*
44	Eccleshill – City – St Enoch's Road Top*
45	Wibsey
46	Buttershaw
47	Little Horton*

*Intermediate turning point of a main service

Service 30 operated as a through cross-city route to services 24/5/6 and vice-versa.

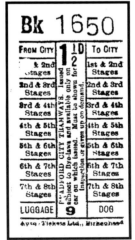

1915 Railless ticket

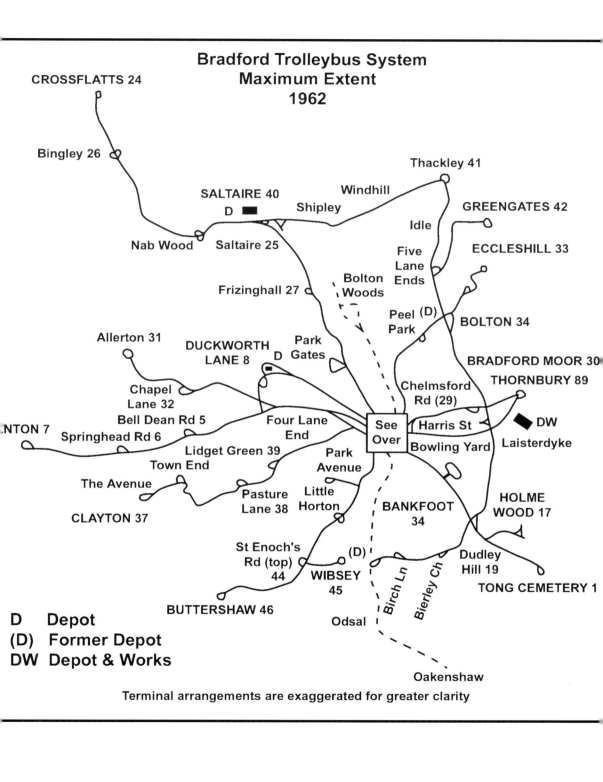

Bradford Trolleybus System
Maximum Extent
1962

CROSSFLATTS 24

Bingley 26

SALTAIRE 40
D

Shipley

Windhill

Thackley 41

GREENGATES 42

Idle

ECCLESHILL 33

Nab Wood   Saltaire 25

Five
Lane
Ends

Frizinghall 27

Bolton
Woods

Peel (D)
Park

BOLTON 34

Allerton 31

DUCKWORTH
LANE 8   D

Park
Gates

Chelmsford
Rd (29)

BRADFORD MOOR 30
THORNBURY 89

Chapel
Lane 32

NTON 7
Springhead Rd 6

Bell Dean Rd 5

Four Lane
End

Lidget Green 39

Town End

See
Over

Harris St

DW

Bowling Yard

Laisterdyke

The Avenue

Pasture
Lane 38

Little
Horton

Park
Avenue

BANKFOOT
34

HOLME
WOOD 17

CLAYTON 37

St Enoch's
Rd (top)
44

(D)

WIBSEY
45

Birch Ln

Bierley Ch

Dudley
Hill 19

TONG CEMETERY 1

BUTTERSHAW 46

Odsal

Oakenshaw

D   Depot
(D)   Former Depot
DW   Depot & Works

Terminal arrangements are exaggerated for greater clarity

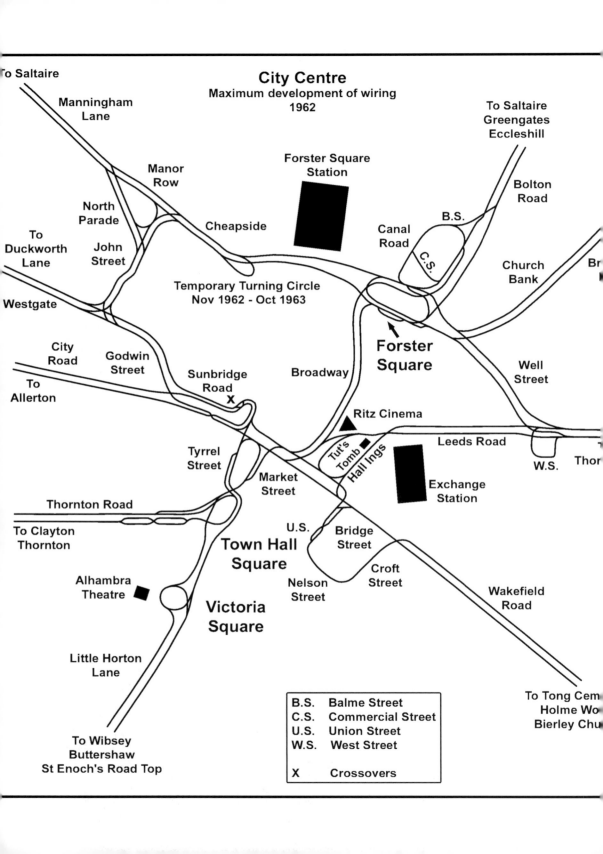

City Centre
Maximum development of wiring
1962

THE RAILLESS YEARS

1.   This is Dudley Hill terminus in Sticker Lane just after the commencement of the railless service to Laisterdyke. No 240, showing the rear platform, is attracting the interest of locals. The railless turning circle crosses the tram wiring of the stub siding for cars turning at Dudley Hill on the Wakefield Road route. No photographs of the other railless, 241, in its original form, appear to exist. (BCT/J.S. King coll.)

2.   Laisterdyke terminus was at the other end of Sticker Lane, just before the junction with Leeds Road. Vehicles drove into Latimer Street, reversed out into Sticker Lane, and transferred poles to the wires on the left to return to Dudley Hill. Some time after the route was extended to Bolton, reversing arrangements here were altered to allow the vehicle to reverse into Latimer Street. This situation lasted until 1934 when the Greenhill Lane reverser was erected at the other side of the Leeds Road junction (see photograph 11). The railless shown turning into Latimer Street is one of the 503-520 Bradford built type, which had started to enter service in mid 1914, just before the route extension to Bolton. (BCT/S. Lockwood coll.)

3.   The original railless cars, 240/241 were renumbered into a railless series as 502/1, and during the First World War were converted into goods vehicles with a capability to operate away from railless routes using battery power, or on tram routes by way of a skate in the track. 502 was a flat lorry, whilst 501 (the former 241), seen here, was a covered wagon and was used to operate a parcels service over the tram route to Leeds. This view shows it in Hall Ings outside the Tramways Department offices, the site that in the 1930s had Britannia House built on it. The Tramways Offices moved to 11 Forster Square, on the corner of Bolton Road, in 1929 and remained there for the rest of the trolleybus era. The presence of a registration number on the vehicle dates this view to 1921 at the earliest. (Keighley News/J.S.King coll.)

4.   Railless 504 is seen at the Cleckheaton Road railway bridge over the Lancashire and Yorkshire Railway on the Oakenshaw service, which opened in October 1914. The single line of overhead is evident. The circumstances depicted are not known. This may be a road accident which has caused the horse drawn cart to spill its load on the causeway, or perhaps the presence of a chauffeured motor car, locally registered, indicates a visit by the Lord Mayor, and that 504 is performing a trial run for civic dignitaries. Whatever the reason it has provided a rare view of the original Oakenshaw installation. 504 was one of the Oakenshaw regulars throughout its life. Over seventy years later, the bridge was adjacent to the short lived 'Transperience' transport themed attraction, which exhibited preserved trolleybuses, including Bradford examples, operating around a circuit of wiring. (BCT/J.S.King coll.)

5.   1915 saw the introduction of the railless to Canal Road with routes to Frizinghall and Bolton Woods. Photographs on these sections are very rare, but this mid 1920s view is of 524 in Canal Road at Railway Cottages on the Frizinghall route. This type of vehicle was introduced in 1923 and was designed for one-man operation. Whilst this was possible on the Frizinghall service, the Bolton Woods route required a conductor to operate the pull frog at Stanley Road junction. These 'one-man' vehicles carried a teak livery instead of the usual dark Prussian blue and cream. Sadly, this photograph was taken following a fatal accident in fog. (J.S.King coll.)

BANKFOOT TO BOLTON

6.   During 1914, the original Dudley Hill to Laisterdyke service was extended at both ends to operate between Bankfoot and Bolton Junction. Unusually for a trolleybus route, it was always a suburban service that did not penetrate the city centre. The route was given the no 34 when numbers were introduced in the early 1930s. This is the Bankfoot turning circle at the junction of Rooley Lane, with Manchester Road running across the foreground of this view. Until 1940, the Oakenshaw trolleybuses ran along Manchester Road but there was never any connection in the overhead wiring between the two routes. Two Karrier vehicles are seen in this 1960 view. On the right is pre–war E4 684 rebodied by Crossley in 1952 and on the left at the terminal stop is Llanelly 777 with a 1956 East Lancs body (also showing the 'Lanry' advertisement). (C.W.Routh)

7.   Running for the trolley - a view of Bankfoot terminus from the opposite direction shows AEC 634 waiting to return to Bolton. This photograph is dated 5th July 1950, shortly after the end of Bradford's trams. These were at this time being broken up in Bankfoot depot just around the corner. In the background can be seen the last remnants of the tram overhead wiring on Manchester Road, which retained the twin wires, a remnant of the Oakenshaw trackless service. 634 was delivered in 1937 as a prototype for the large batch of AEC trolleybuses which arrived in 1938. It was rebodied by East Lancs in 1956.
(A.D.Packer/J.Copland)

8.   At Birch Lane, near the junction of Rooley Lane and Rooley Avenue, a turning circle was erected just after the Second World War. This was used for special workings in connection with sports events at Odsal Stadium. Two loops, one in each direction, were also provided to store trolleybuses on these workings. This view shows a line-up headed by BUT 745 in the westbound loop on 29th September 1951. This loop was later removed but the other one and the turning circle remained for use until the route was abandoned. This area is now an extremely busy motorway interchange, where Bradford's motorway link to the M62 and M1 commences. Note that a chock has been placed in front of the offside wheel of 745, in accordance with regulations when a vehicle was left unattended. The chock was attached by chain to the cab. (A.D.Packer/J.Copland)

9.   Further towards Dudley Hill, at Bierley Church, another turning circle was provided. This did not see significant use until the end of 1956 when a peak hour service was introduced from the city centre via Dudley Hill. Prompted by the Suez fuel crisis, this service was intended to reduce motorbus mileage. It required two vehicles, one of which was usually the ex Darlington single decker, T403. This was one of two of this type that

had been stored in working order after purchase in 1954. (The other, T404, had been scrapped before 1957). The service must have proved worthwhile as it continued after the crisis and lasted, albeit with reduced frequency, until 1963. No route number was initially allocated but it was given the number 16 in the early 1960s. T403, seen on this service on 23rd February 1957, has turned on the circle and is waiting to return to City. Bierley Church itself can be seen in the left background. (A.D.Packer/J.Copland)

10.　　At Dudley Hill, service 34 crossed the Wakefield Road services to Tong Cemetery and Holme Wood. In 1956, trolleybuses proceeding towards Bankfoot were rerouted into Mulcott Road where a loop was provided so that Wakefield Road trolleybuses turning short at Dudley Hill could wait clear of the 34 service wires. Notts & Derby AEC 588, with 1958 East Lancs body, is in Mulcott Road preparing to turn right into Wakefield Road. From there it will turn left into Rooley Lane towards Bankfoot. (S.Lockwood coll.)

11.　　Between Dudley Hill and Laisterdyke, service 34 followed the original 1911 railless route along Sticker Lane. The site of the first terminus at Laisterdyke is seen here at the junction with Leeds Road, where there were depot connections to and from the Bolton direction. Despite there being other depots very close to both termini of the 34 route, it was always worked from Thornbury, which was about a mile from Laisterdyke. In the 1930s the original reverser at Latimer Street (situated behind the camera in this view) was moved across the junction to Greenhill Lane. Vehicles entering or leaving service to and from Bankfoot or the Wakefield Road routes had to use this reverser as there was no direct access wiring from Thornbury depot to and from the Sticker Lane direction. Jo'burg Sunbeam MF2 699 with 1956 East Lancs body has just negotiated the crossings at this point in September 1960. In the background can be seen the Leeds Road wiring, the connection from Leeds Road towards Bolton, and just beyond that the Greenhill Lane reverser – one of only three on the system at this time. In the very far distance one of the white gables of the Barrack Tavern is visible (see photograph 13). (C.W.Routh)

12.　　This is Laisterdyke near the end of the war showing English Electric single decker 570 loading at the Laisterdyke stop for Bankfoot. This is probably a special working for a sports event at Odsal Stadium. The position of the booms indicates that the trolleybus has just used the Greenhill Lane reverser. Note the wartime markings on the vehicle. (J.A.Pitts)

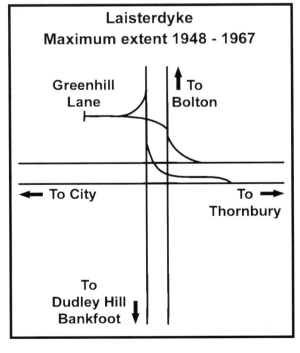

Laisterdyke
Maximum extent 1948 - 1967

Greenhill Lane

↑ To Bolton

← To City

To → Thornbury

To Dudley Hill Bankfoot ↓

13.   The next section of route ran along Killinghall Road and crossed the Bradford Moor service at the Barrack Tavern. Up to 1960 this was a plain crossing but then a connection was provided from the Bradford Moor direction towards Laisterdyke. This had a two-fold purpose. Firstly, it allowed trolleybuses entering service from Thornbury Depot towards Bankfoot to do so without having to negotiate the Greenhill Lane reverser. Secondly, it created a testing circuit for trolleybuses that had received mechanical attention in Thornbury works, this being routed via Bradford Moor terminus, Barrack Tavern, Laisterdyke and Thornbury. The circuit was available for use right up to the end of trolleybus operations. Karrier 720, with 1958 East Lancs body, calls at the stop in 1964 with the connection from Bradford Moor and the Barrack Tavern both evident behind the vehicle. (J.S.King)

14.   666 meets 222. Having passed through the Undercliffe area and crossed Harrogate Road the service 34 route arrived at Bolton Junction, probably the most complex wiring lay-out on the system outside the city centre. Here the 34s turned by way of a one-way anti-clockwise loop around Undercliffe Road, Bolton Road, Idle Road and Pelham Road. The terminal stop was in Idle Road adjacent to the main junction where the 40/42 Saltaire/Greengates routes branched off the Eccleshill route. Originally when the service was extended from Laisterdyke in 1914, the loop was clockwise. From 1964, when route 34 was abandoned, all the wiring between this point and Dudley Hill was retained for use by vehicles needing access to and from Thornbury depot. Seen at the terminal stop waiting to return to Bankfoot is 1939 AEC 666, looking most un-beastlike with its handsome 1956 East Lancs body. By the time of this view (post 1960) the trailing frogs of the connection from the Idle routes (40/42) had been moved up to allow trolleybuses returning to depot to pass unhindered any service 34 vehicle standing at the terminus. Note that the photographer has, by coincidence, caught another vehicle displaying numerical symmetry in this shot–a Bradford City Dennis F12 fire engine registered JKY 222. (J.Fozard/R.F.Mack)

15.　The Clayton route opened in September 1926 and operated as far as Town End. It was allocated the service number 37 in the early 1930s. In July 1956 an extension of just over half a mile was opened along The Avenue. Here AEC 630 with 1947 Northern Coachbuilders body is seen at the turning circle framed by traction poles and a gas lamp. This extension lasted until May 1970 when a bus route reorganisation in the area resulted in the route being cut back to the original terminus at Town End. (C.W.Routh)

Section	Mins. Service	From City	Mins. Service	To City
Clayton				
		MONDAY to FRIDAY		
		4.53 a.m.		5.10 a.m.
	8	5.45 ,, to 6.57 a.m.	8	6.4 ,, to 7.0 a.m.
	6	7.6 ,, ,, 8.48 ,,	6	7.9 ,, ,, 9.3 ,,
	12	8.48 ,, ,, 11.48 ,,	12	9.3 ,, ,, 12.3 p.m.
	6	11.48 ,, ,, 2.12 p.m.	6	12.3 p.m. ,, 2.27 ,,
	8	2.12 p.m. ,, 4.20 ,,	8	2.31 ,, ,, 4.39 ,,
	5	4.20 ,, ,, 6.30 ,,	5	4.39 ,, ,, 6.44 ,,
	12	6.30 ,, ,, 10.54 ,,	12	6.55 ,, ,, 11.19 ,,
		SATURDAY		
		4.53 a.m.		5.10 6.4 a.m.
	15	5.45 ,, to 7.0 a.m.	15	6.24 a.m. to 7.24 a.m.
	10	7.0 ,, ,, 7.40 ,,	10	7.24 ,, ,, 7.54 ,,
	6	7.48 ,, ,, 8.30 ,,	6	8.3 ,, ,, 8.45 ,,
	10	8.30 ,, ,, 11.30 ,,	10	8.52 ,, ,, 11.42 ,,
	6	11.30 ,, ,, 11.0 p.m.	6	11.51 ,, ,, 11.21 p.m.
		SUNDAY		
	20	9.20 a.m. to 1.20 p.m.	20	9.39 a.m. to 1.39 p.m.
	10	1.20 p.m. ,, 10.50 ,,	10	1.54 p.m. ,, 11.14 ,,

16.　　The original terminus at Clayton Town End is shown here. It was also known as The Wells or The Black Bull. When first opened in 1926, Clayton was outside the Bradford boundary and the route was subject to severe competition from West Yorkshire buses which lasted until 1932. Until double deckers were allowed onto the route in 1937, it was also operated for a time as a through service to Oakenshaw. This sylvan scene in 1970 shows St Helens BUT 795 turning after the extension to The Avenue had been abandoned. The terminal stop, outside the Black Bull, is in the background. The wiring up the Avenue goes off to the right, and although the overhead was retained until the whole route closed in July 1971, it was not available for use. (S.Lockwood)

Auto-Tickets L... Birkenhead

PA 65845

Bradford City Transport

3d Issued subject to Bye-laws and Regs. Not Transferable.

ORD. CHILD E.M.F.

17.   In the bleak midwinter - after negotiating the streets of Clayton village, trolleybuses crossed the bridge overlooking Clayton station and turned into Pasture Lane, which ran parallel to a railway embankment. This snowy scene shows AEC 624 with post-war Northern Coachbuilders body negotiating Pasture Lane towards Clayton on 16th January 1955. (J.S.King)

18.   At the other end of Pasture Lane there was a railway bridge over the road, and this prevented double deck operation to Clayton until the road was lowered in 1937. The railway was the Great Northern line from Bradford to Halifax and Keighley, which lost its passenger service in 1955 and finally closed to freight traffic in 1965, by which time the line only ran as far as Thornton. AEC 603, in special livery to celebrate the 1961 Trolleybus Jubilee, has just passed under the bridge en route to City. There were two other locations on the system where trolleybuses passed under railway bridges, these being at Shipley on the Saltaire (40) route and Wakefield Road on the 17/18 services. (J.S.King)

19.   Following a short steep incline from the bridge the Pasture Lane short working turning point was reached. Originally there was a short-lived reversing triangle here where trolleybuses drove into Scholemoor Avenue and reversed out. This was replaced by a conventional turning loop as seen here. The circle saw its busiest period of use after 1951 and there were regular turns here right up until the end of trolleybus operation

in July 1971. On the right BUT 740 waits to return to City after using the circle, whilst on the left Jo'burg 698 with 1956 East Lancs body pauses before turning down Pasture Lane on a Clayton working. Note the emergency door beside the entrance. This was necessary due to the vehicle having been designed to incorporate a platform door although only no 701 of the rebodied Jo'burgs actually had this fitted. (R.F.Mack)

20.   Until 1934, the Clayton trolleybuses ran in parallel with the Lidget Green tram service as far as Beckside Road. When the tram service was abandoned in 1934, a turning facility was provided for trolleybuses here and this was used with lessening frequency until 1963. The loop was dismantled in early 1965. Originally taking the tram service 4, the vehicles turning at Lidget Green were numbered 39 from 1938. This late 1950s view shows Llanelly 782 about to turn on the loop amongst the snow and slush. The rear of a utility Karrier can be seen heading towards City. (J.S.King)

BOLTON—BANKFOOT

Bankfoot (1)								
2	Rooley Lane (19)							
2	2	Bierley Church (18)						
3	2	2	Dudley Hill (17)					
4	3	2	2	Broad Lane (16)				
4	4	3	2	2	Laisterdyke (15)			
5	4	4	3	2	2	Second Avenue (14)		
5	5	4	4	3	2	2	Undercliffe (13)	
5	5	5	4	4	3	2	2	Bolton (12)

ALLERTON

21. The Allerton tram route was converted to trolleybus operation in 1929. This was the first tram to trolleybus conversion in the City and also the first route where double deckers were provided as the norm. The terminus was at the 'country' end of the village in Prune Park Lane at the junction with Stony Lane. From here, on clear days, there was a panoramic vista over the Aire valley. This view from the mid 1950s shows Notts and Derby 589 at the terminal stop having negotiated the turning circle. These vehicles were regulars on the route in both their original and rebodied form until 1960. The route was service 31 until 1966, when it was changed to 16 so as to be in line with motorbus services in the area. (P.Watson)

22. Having dropped down through Allerton village, the route turned sharp left at Chapel Lane where there was a tight intermediate turning loop at the road junction. Karrier 736 is seen unloading passengers here in March 1965 whilst operating a tea-time extra journey to Chapel Lane, which was service 32. In the last years of the route this circle was rarely used. (A.D.Packer/J.Copland)

23.   The Allerton service joined the Thornton route at Four Lane Ends. From 1958, a one–way system of wiring was adopted here with inbound trolleybuses from Allerton being diverted via West Park Road onto Thornton Road. There was also a connection to provide a turning facility using the one–way wiring. Mexborough Sunbeam 842 is heading up Allerton Road with West Park Road in the background. The vehicle has just cleared the interlaced frogs of the depot connection up Squire Lane to the left. Curiously for Bradford, there was never a direct wiring link to allow trolleybuses from the Allerton direction, running to depot, to turn left into Squire Lane, such vehicles having to go round the entire one-way wiring to gain access. (See wiring diagram below photograph 37.) This view was taken on 27th February 1971, the last day of public service on the Allerton route. It was also the first week that decimal fares were charged, Bradford being one of only two trolleybus systems to last into the decimal coinage era, the other being the Teesside system, which closed in April 1971. (S.Lockwood)

24.   The next series of tram to trolleybus conversions centred on the Bolton Road corridor out from the city centre. The first to be converted was the long indirect route to Saltaire (6.5 miles/10.5km) via Idle, Thackley and Shipley, which opened for trolleybuses in March 1930. The terminus was at the junction of Saltaire Road and Keighley Road near the Saltaire tram depot and originally the turning circle was kept away from the tram wires. Later, a roundabout was installed which provided the terminus for the 40 and the Saltaire (25) service via Manningham Lane, which became trolleybus operated during 1939. Just short of the roundabout there was a triangular reverser into Dove Street for use in emergencies. This saw very infrequent use but did survive right up to the last day of the service in June 1971, as did a loop of wiring into Saltaire Depot, again for emergency purposes. Park Royal utility Karrier 720 stands at the terminal stop on the left in 1951 whilst similar vehicle 718 approaches from the Shipley direction. The Dove Street reverser wiring is on the right. (C.W.Routh)

25.   This is Shipley town centre, showing English Electric six wheeler 592, a type that was the mainstay of the route in its early days. The vehicle has just passed Fox Corner junction on its way to Saltaire in this late 1930s view of Briggate. Despite Shipley being quite a large community, there was never any provision for trolleybuses to turn here. (J.S.King coll.)

26.   The outer end of service 40 lay outside the Bradford boundary and within Shipley Urban District Council's area. The route crossed into Bradford west of Thackley Corner, where trolleybuses turned right from Leeds Road towards Idle and Bolton. Here, a complete circle of wiring was provided to allow vehicles to turn back from either direction. At one time, for instance, there was a regular schools working between Thackley Corner and Crossflatts via Saltaire. This view shows BUT 758 on an enthusiasts' tour (facing the direction of Bolton) in February 1966 with the complete circle in the background. 758 had been stored out of service with most others of this type since 1964 and had just been reinstated into traffic together with 753 and 757. This vehicle remained in service until July 1971, by which time it had become the last rear entrance trolleybus in public service in Britain. It survives at the Trolleybus Museum at Sandtoft although it is unrestored. The destination shown is spurious and would not have been displayed on a Bradford trolleybus in normal circumstances. (A.D.Packer/J.Copland)

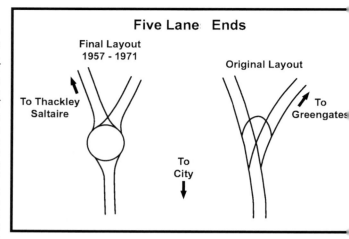

Five Lane Ends

Final Layout
1957 - 1971

Original Layout

To Thackley Saltaire

To Greengates

To City

27.   At Five Lane Ends, the Saltaire route met the 1½ mile/2.4km branch from Greengates. The turning loop provided here can be seen in the background of this April 1956 view. The following year, a roundabout was constructed here, and a full circle of wiring provided around it, allowing turns from any direction. AEC 612, with utility Brush body, has negotiated the junction on its way from Greengates. In the background on the left can be seen the large 'Tramway Shelter' and on the right is the light coloured building of the International Harvester tractor works. This was formerly the premises of the Jowett motor factory where 'Javelin' cars and 'Bradford' vans were made. (A.D.Packer/J.Copland)

GREENGATES

28.   The Greengates section replaced the Idle tram route in March 1931 and was later allocated service number 42. The terminus was on a one-way loop around Albion Road and Leeds Road. Standing at the terminal stop in Albion Road beside the mill (with Leeds Road in the background looking towards Greengates junction) is AEC 639. This vehicle was unique in that it was rebodied in 1956 with a second hand Northern Coachbuilders body formerly used on 1935 AEC 618 (see photograph 33). (A.D.Packer/J.Copland)

29.   Bolton Junction was a major trolleybus intersection, and was adjacent to Bolton depot which provided vehicles for the Bolton Road routes until the depot closed in 1958. Here, the Saltaire/Greengates routes diverged from the Eccleshill service and it was also the terminus for the radial route to Bankfoot (see photograph 14). The complicated wiring necessary at this point is shown here in the left background as rebodied Notts and Derby 593 negotiates the turn from Idle Road into Bolton Road heading towards City. The Eccleshill wires continue into the background, and the service 34 terminus is on the right. The link wires for Thornbury depot workings cross the view from left to right. (J.Fozard/R.F.Mack)

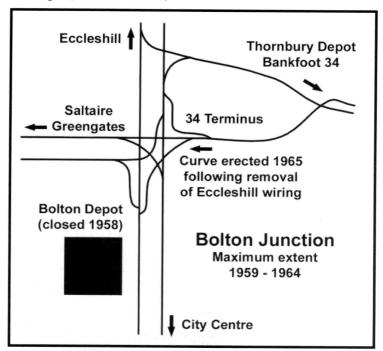

Eccleshill ↑

Thornbury Depot
Bankfoot 34

Saltaire
← Greengates

34 Terminus

←
Curve erected 1965
following removal
of Eccleshill wiring

Bolton Depot
(closed 1958)

Bolton Junction
Maximum extent
1959 - 1964

↓ City Centre

ECCLESHILL

30.   Two Bradfords and a Darlington. The remaining Bolton Road service was the short route to Eccleshill which replaced the tram service in June 1934. The tram route number 33 was retained. Originally, until 1941, trolleybuses turned into Moorside Road (off to the right) and reversed out. The route was originally the regular haunt of the English Electric single deck vehicles. It is apt, therefore, that this 1957 view of the original Eccleshill terminus at the Mechanics Institute shows the short lived Darlington single decker T403 on tour, together with indigenous AEC 642 and a Jowett 'Bradford' van made not very far away in Idle. Later that year, a cross-city service was introduced from Eccleshill to St Enoch's Road Top and this was numbered 44. (C.W.Routh)

31.   One of the last extensions to the Bradford system, and probably the most spectacular, occurred in August 1959, when a half mile section was opened from the Mechanics Institute to Faltis Square, situated on the fringe of the Thorpe Edge housing estate. This involved traversing tight curves in narrow village streets and culminated in a severely graded section of 1 in 8, the steepest on the system, down The Bank to a turning circle around Faltis Square. Special attention was given to the erection, positioning and maintenance of the overhead wiring on The Bank to minimise the risk of dewirements. Hastings Sunbeam 811 is seen loading at the terminus before tackling the gradient in 1963. This extension had a very short life, the all day service being withdrawn in late 1962 (including all the cross-city 44 journeys) with a residual peak hours only provision lasting until final abandonment in October 1964. (A.D.Packer/J.Copland)

Notice No. 2894
2nd January, 1969

NOTICE TO DRIVERS AND
CONDUCTORS
REPOSITIONING OF PULL FROG
IDLE ROAD – BOLTON
JUNCTION

In connection with the installation of Traffic Signals at Bolton Junction, the Pull Frog in Idle Road for buses proceeding from the direction of Five Lane Ends towards Laisterdyke is to be moved away from the junction to a point near to the Section Insulators at Pole No.102, Idle Road. This will enable buses to be on the correct wiring before reaching the traffic signals.
It is anticipated that this arrangement will be in operation as from Sunday, 5th January, 1969.

E. Deakin
General Manager

32. From Bolton Junction towards City, Bolton Road steadily descends until Forster Square is reached in the city centre itself. At the junction with Lister Lane, a short-working turning circle was provided principally to serve events at the nearby Peel Park. Interestingly, it was the last example in Bradford of narrow (18 inches/457mm) spaced wiring. Note how the wires taper out above the vehicle from 18 inches wide to the normal 2 feet/609mm configura-tion. In later years its use was very rare and the circle was removed altogether in 1967. This 1961 view shows St Helens BUT 794 on an early morning working which turned here, and then worked through the city centre to Bradford Moor. In June 1970, the poor condition of the Bolton Road wiring resulted in a 20mph/32km/h speed restriction being imposed between Peel Park and Five Lane Ends. The affected section in Bolton Road was renewed as far as Bolton Junction in September using an overhead crew hired from Huddersfield Corporation, whose own trolleybus system had been closed since July 1968. (J.S.King)

33. Further down Bolton Road, the route overlooked the valley allowing a panoramic view of an industrial landscape. This included Bradford's electricity power station as seen in this view. Whilst power for the trolleybus system within the city came from here, the portions of route in the Shipley and Bingley areas were fed from the National Grid. Passing in the foreground, City bound, is Darlington Karrier 785 with 1958 East Lancs front entrance bodywork. This was the vehicle that formerly ran in Bradford in single deck form as T403 (see photographs 9,30 and 70). (J.S.King)

34. This is a view of 1950s Bradford including pubs, mills and trolleybuses. It shows Bolton Road bottom at Cross Sun Street on the edge of the city centre. On the left, AEC 662 is leaving the city, passing Karrier E4 687 on the right. Note the wiring is suspended from bracket arms, a feature that continued up Bolton Road from this point.(J.S.King)

THORNTON

35.   The route along Thornton Road to Thornton village was almost 5 miles in length and was numbered service 7. It terminated at the far side of the village at Thornton Cemetery, where a turning circle was provided. Until 1965, the service ran to the city centre only, but from then until closure, it was operated as a cross-city route to Thornbury. AEC 618 is shown at the terminus in 1954, with a Notts and Derby AEC behind. 618 was withdrawn in 1956 and its 1947 Northern Coachbuilders body transferred to 1938 AEC 639 (see photograph 28). (R.F.Mack)

36.   At the Bradford end of the village, a turning facility was provided early in the Second World War at Springhead Road, where a wide road junction was used to accommodate a turning circle. Journeys terminating here showed service 6 and there were regular scheduled turns until February 1971, when most of these were withdrawn. Darlington Karrier 787 shows off its front entrance as it turns here. (Travel Lens Photographic)

37.   Further turning facilities were provided at Bell Dean Road and this was initially numbered 6, becoming 5 after the Springhead Road loop was brought into use. A complete circle of wiring was provided with connections from both the Thornton and City directions. For this reason, the trolleybus driving school used it frequently and AEC 060, formerly 597 in the passenger fleet, is seen at the loop in the early 1960s. Bradford was unusual in allocating trolleybuses for the sole use of driver training, even re-numbering them in the ancillary vehicle fleet. Following the introduction of a new motorbus service into the area in 1964, the Bell Dean turning loop lost its scheduled workings and the wiring was removed altogether in March 1965. (J.Fozard/R.F.Mack)

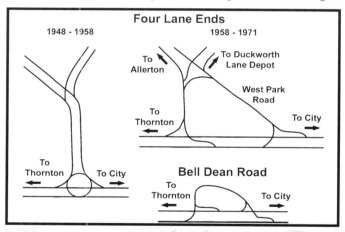

38.   Four Lane Ends was the junction of the Allerton and Thornton routes. Until 1958 there was a full circle of wiring here allowing turns from any direction. The introduction of the rebodied Darlingtons, with their longer bodies, raised doubts as to their suitability to negotiate this circle. Arrangements were made to abolish it by introducing a one-way wiring system, which involved the erection of wiring in West Park Road (see photograph 23). The pre-1958 circle can be seen in this view of Notts and Derby AEC 585 crossing the junction en route, despite the destination being displayed, to Thornton. (J.S.King)

DUCKWORTH LANE

39. The service 8 Duckworth Lane route was possibly the best remembered of all Bradford's trolleybus services and one to which trolleybus operation was ideally suited. It was a short (2 miles) route with an intensive service frequency (up to every 2 minutes at peak hours). Added to this the route included one of the steepest gradients on the system at Whetley Hill (1 in 9.7). Running time from the city centre was 10 minutes with 9 minutes allowed for the return journey. The terminus, seen here, was at a tight turning circle opposite Bradford Royal Infirmary. The wiring continued beyond the terminus, turning left down Squire Lane to connect with the Allerton wires near Four Lane Ends. This link was brought into use in 1947 for vehicles running to and from Duckworth Lane depot. Two of the latter-day mainstays of the route, the rebodied front entrance Karriers, are seen at the terminus in March 1962, headed by 725. The AEC motorbus is on the no 80 Lister Park–Heaton–Bankfoot service. (A.D.Packer/J.Copland)

40. The depot was at the other end of Duckworth Lane and was at the original terminus of the route in 1935. The following year, a half-mile extension along Duckworth Lane to the Infirmary was opened. This 1950s view shows utility Karrier 735 having reversed out of the depot to take up service. This vehicle was, at that time, Thornbury based, and so is probably working a Sunday afternoon hospital special. To get to Duckworth Lane terminus it would have to negotiate the Toller Lane/Little Lane loop behind the depot and emerge onto Duckworth Lane using the right turn wiring out of Little Lane which can be seen in the background. The connection was removed in 1956 following the building of a roundabout at the nearby Duckworth Lane/Toller Lane junction. This gave an opportunity to include a wiring link to allow trolleybuses a more direct routeing from the depot to the terminus (see photograph 43). (J.Fozard)

41. Access to Duckworth Lane depot from the city centre direction was via the one-way wiring behind the depot on Toller Lane and Little Lane. This was the original Duckworth Lane service terminal loop. Seen in Toller Lane, returning to depot during the last week of trolleybus operation in March 1972, is Mexborough 845. Note that the 'Trolley Bus Stop' still existed on the left even though there was no regular service along this part of Toller Lane. (A.D.Packer/J.Copland)

42.   The old order changeth. This is downtown Duckworth Lane in May 1959, just after the first of the rebodied Karriers with front entrances had appeared. Passengers make to board at the front of 725, one of the first to enter service, whilst the old guard, represented by 597, the first of the 1934 AEC vehicles (rebodied by Northern Coachbuilders after the war) waits behind. Within a year Duckworth Lane depot would have a 100% front entrance fleet and 597 would be transferred to Thornbury for its last two years of public service. The depot itself is situated behind 597. (J.S.King)

43.   The Duckworth Lane/Toller Lane junction roundabout is seen here showing the wiring enabling vehicles from the depot to turn back towards the terminus. The roundabout was remodelled in 1961 and this connection moved further towards Duckworth Lane. In the meantime another connection had been provided in December 1960 for late running vehicles to turn back towards City. This was known as the Whitby Road loop after the adjacent side road. Although very rarely used it remained until the end of the system. This view was taken during the few months that both loops existed together and shows rebodied Karrier 731 travelling inbound to City. (J.S.King)

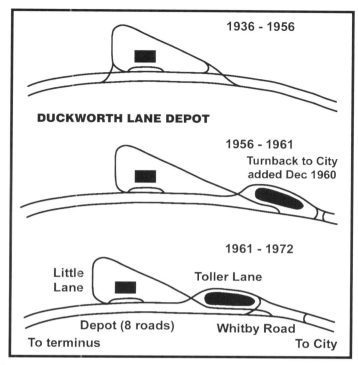

1936 - 1956

DUCKWORTH LANE DEPOT

1956 - 1961
Turnback to City added Dec 1960

1961 - 1972

Little Lane

Toller Lane

Depot (8 roads)

Whitby Road

To terminus

To City

44. This part of Toller Lane was an attractive tree lined dual carriageway. It was the scene of two instances of trolleybuses overturning, both involving utility Brush bodied vehicles. The first occasion, shown here, was in 1948 when 612 came to grief opposite the Elite and Coliseum cinemas which stood at the top of Fairbank Road. 612 later returned to service. In 1953, 599 overturned whilst travelling in the opposite direction. The damage was such that it was withdrawn from service immediately. (Telegraph and Argus)

45.   At the lower end of Toller Lane, the route dropped sharply towards the city centre down Whetley Hill, one of the steepest on the system. Seen making the ascent, with a view looking towards the city centre and White Abbey Road at the bottom of the hill, is rebodied Karrier 710. This scene is dated 5th September 1971. (A.D.Packer/J.Copland)

Notice No. 3326
8th September, 1971

NOTICE TO ALL SUPERVISORY STAFF
BOTH ENGINEERING AND TRAFFIC

TROLLEYBUS OPERATION

In view of the fact that Bradford is now the sole operator of trolley vehicles in this Country there are increasing pressures from trolleybus enthusiasts to be allowed to drive or have unofficial contacts with these vehicles.

May I make it perfectly clear that unless an individual obtains authority from me he is not, under any circumstances, to be allowed on depot premises or to handle or travel on a trolley vehicle in any other position than as a normal passenger.

E.Deakin
General Manager

TONG CEMETERY
AND
HOLME WOOD

46.   The end of the line. The route 18 Wakefield Road trolleybus service ended at Tong Cemetery – was there ever a more grim sounding trolleybus terminus? This point was at the city boundary where the tram service had divided to continue to Birkenshaw or Drighlington. The wide road junction enabled a turning circle to be provided and in August 1966 Jo'burg 697 is seen in mid-turn. In the background is Tong Comprehensive School and the cemetery itself is behind the camera. (S.Lockwood)

47.   The final route extension to the Bradford system was a ¾-mile spur off the Tong Cemetery route via Knowles Lane into the developing Holme Wood housing estate. This opened on 6th March 1960 and was allocated service number 17, which had last been used for the tram service to Birkenshaw. The road layout within the estate necessitated the use of a reversing triangle at the terminus, a device that the Transport Department had tried to avoid throughout the history of the system. This was situated at the junction with Dorchester Crescent. Llanelly 783 pauses at the end of the wires before reversing on the last day of the trolleybus service, 1st April 1967. Note the contrast in 1960s fashion – cloth caps and a mini-skirt. (J.S.King).

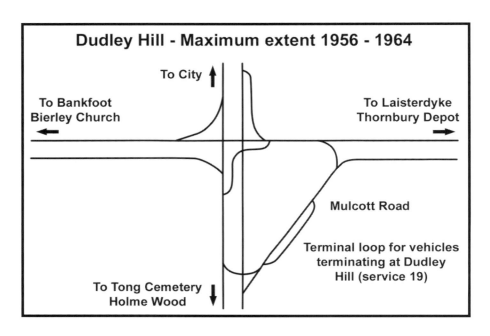

Dudley Hill - Maximum extent 1956 - 1964

To City ↑

To Bankfoot
Bierley Church
←

To Laisterdyke
Thornbury Depot
→

Mulcott Road

Terminal loop for vehicles
terminating at Dudley
Hill (service 19)

To Tong Cemetery
Holme Wood ↓

48.   The junction at Dudley Hill was a major trolleybus intersection and it is seen at its maximum state of development (post 1956). This view looks in the direction of the city centre with Wakefield Road in the foreground, Rooley Lane on the left and Sticker Lane on the right. Brighton 802 is at the lights waiting to proceed to Holme Wood. Points to note are: the long lead for the left turn between Wakefield Road and Sticker Lane used by vehicles turning short at Dudley Hill; the interlaced frog in the foreground leading into Sticker Lane for depot journeys, and the curve from Rooley Lane left into Wakefield Road towards the city centre used for the Bierley Church service. (J.S.King)

CROSSFLATTS

49.   The Crossflatts terminus was situated between Bingley and Keighley in the Aire Valley, at the end of a seven mile route from the city centre and about three miles from Keighley. Trolleybuses swung across the wide A650 road to turn as shown by Darlington 787 on 13th July 1963. The service was number 24. From 1950 the route was operated as a cross-city service to Bradford Moor until the latter route was closed in November 1962. (J.S.King)

50.   The turning facility at Bingley was at Bingley Church, at the Crossflatts end of the town centre, where a turning circle enabled short working journeys (service 26) to turn and stand clear of the through wires. Most of the wiring between Bingley and Crossflatts was constructed using experimental American Ohio Brass fittings, and the neat construction of the turning circle is evident here as BUT 754 (with a rather battered front dash panel) passes through en route to Crossflatts. Every trolleybus operating in the Bingley Urban District Council area (and also the drivers) had to have a separate Hackney Carriage licence issued by the council. (J.S.King)

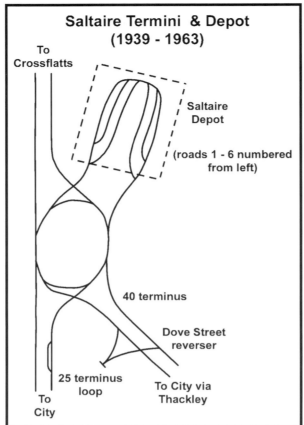

Saltaire Termini & Depot
(1939 - 1963)

To Crossflatts

Saltaire Depot

(roads 1 - 6 numbered from left)

40 terminus

Dove Street reverser

25 terminus loop

To City via Thackley

To City

51.   The route between Bingley and Saltaire followed the Aire Valley, crossing the River Aire at Cottingley Bridge. At Nab Wood there was a turning point at the Bingley UDC/ Shipley UDC boundary (see photograph 105). A short distance from Nab Wood was Saltaire, where the depot for the route was situated. The roundabout outside the depot formed the terminus of the service 40 trolleybus via Thackley as well as the turning point for short workings on the Crossflatts route (service 25). This view is of an early wartime scene showing Saltaire depot. Keighley Road, heading towards Bingley is at the left hand side of the building. AECs 668 and 661, from the large batch which formed the initial Saltaire depot alloation, are seen in wartime guise with white edging and hooded destination indicators. Unlike many of its sisters 668 was never rebodied and was one of the last to survive in original form when withdrawn at the end of 1959. It was stored as a possible preservation project but was eventually scrapped in 1962. Note also the hoods over the skates on the overhead wiring frogs - this was another wartime precaution to hide any sparking. (A.D.Parker coll.).

52.   Just beyond the city boundary, at Ashfield Avenue, a very tight turning circle was erected in 1944. This was known as Frizinghall and was allocated service number 27. There were scheduled turns here at peak hours and on Saturday mornings, often operating through to Chelmsford Road on the Bradford Moor route. The circle, situated in the mouth of Ashfield Road, can be seen behind the vehicle. The trolleybus is Notts and Derby BUT 769, which entered service at the time of the Queen's Coronation in 1953 in a special livery of light blue, red and cream. Sister vehicle 764 was similarly adorned, though in a different style. The legend below the windscreen reads 'Long live the Queen'. (S.Lockwood coll.)

53.   One of the more obscure locations on the Bradford trolleybus system was the 'Park Gates' turning loop. This left the Crossflatts route at Lister Park gates and formed a one-way loop via Oak Lane, St Mary's Road and North Park Road. It was used principally to turn special journeys for Bradford City AFC home games at Valley Parade (just off Manningham Lane). Llanelly Karrier 775 is seen in this attractive view of North Park Road in the late 1950's. (J.S.King)

54.   In late 1960, the awkward-to-use Frizinghall loop was effectively replaced by this turning circle within the Park Gates loop situated off Manningham Lane in Oak Lane. This new facility also proved problematical and drivers had great difficulty in turning here during the dark. Its regular use lasted only a month before the use

of the Frizinghall circle was resumed. Notts and Derby BUT 764 has a go during an enthusiasts tour in 1963. The Park Gates loop wires can be seen trailing in from North Park Road on the right of this view. (J.S.King)

55.   One of the best remembered shops in Bradford was Busby's department store at the city centre end of Manningham Lane. This is the scene in June 1953 with the store dressed for the Queen's Coronation and BUT 756 displaying a front decoration which many trolleybuses carried during the period of celebrations. The vehicle is in its original livery with grey roof. Busby's later became a branch of Debenham's and the building was destroyed by fire in 1979. (A.D.Packer/J.Copland)

Section	Mins. Service	From City	Mins. Service	To City
Crossflatts		MONDAY to FRIDAY		
	12	5.38 a.m. to 4.26 p.m.	12	5.40 a.m. to 6.52 a.m.
	6	4.26 p.m. ,, 6.14 ,,	12	7.3 ,, ,, 4.51 p.m.
	12	6.14 ,, ,, 10.50 ,,	6	4.51 p.m. ,, 6.39 ,,
			12	6.39 ,, ,, 10.39 ,,
				10.44* 10.56* 11.8* ,,
				11.20* p.m.
		SATURDAY		
		5.5 a.m.		
	12	5.38 a.m. to 10.50 p.m.	12	5.39 a.m. to 10.39 p.m.
				10.44* 10.56* 11.8* ,,
				11.20* p.m.
		SUNDAY		
	15	10.2 a.m. to 1.17 p.m.	15	9.35 a.m. to 1.20 p.m.
	12	1.26 p.m. ,, 10.50 ,,	12	1.27 p.m. ,, 10.39 ,,
				10.44* 10.56* 11.8* ,,
				11.20* p.m.
				* To Saltaire only

BRADFORD MOOR

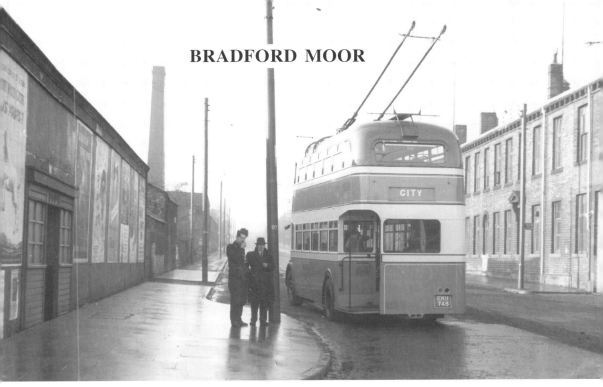

56.   On Sunday, 4th December 1949, the temporary motorbus service to Bradford Moor, which had replaced the trams earlier in the year, was itself replaced by trolleybuses. This is the first public service journey standing at the Bradford Moor terminus on Leeds Old Road with brand new BUT 748. Note the passenger waiting room. A loop in the wiring was erected here in 1958 to allow vehicles to overtake. The destination indicator on the rear of trolleybuses lasted until the mid 1950s after which the aperture was altered to show a service number. (J.A.Pitts)

57.   After intersecting the Bolton-Bankfoot wires at the Barrack Tavern, the Bradford Moor wires crossed into Barkerend Road. At the junction with Chelmsford Road there was a turning circle in the wide road junction. Given the service number 29, few vehicles could show this and most displayed route 27 allocated to the Frizinghall turn. On 14th March 1959, BUT 801, the first St Helens vehicle to enter service, turns here on the Saturday morning service through to Frizinghall. (J.S.King)

58.   Near to the city centre, wires were erected along Harris Street to create a diversionary route between Barkerend Road and Leeds Road in case the steep Church Bank became impassable. Within a year of the Bradford Moor route opening, this link became invaluable when a major building fire in Forster Square caused severe damage to trolleybus wiring. Trolleybuses were unable to use Forster Square for two months and the Bradford Moor route terminated at Hall Ings, using the Harris Street link to access Leeds Road. On 10th June 1950, two days after the fire, BUT 749 turns into Harris Street from Barkerend Road on an inward journey to the city centre. Note the disused tram track. (J.Copland)

59.   The Bradford Moor service left Forster Square from the city centre via Church Bank, one of the steepest gradients on the system. Notts and Derby 764 is seen tackling the ascent. This vehicle was one of the type fitted during its stay at Bradford with modernised destination indicators replacing the original Notts and Derby layout. (J.S.King)

THORNBURY

60.   In 1952 the number 89 Thornbury motorbus service was converted to trolleybus operation following an upgrade of the wiring, which had previously only been used for depot workings. The route shared the same terminus as the Bradford Moor service at the roundabout at Thornbury. The 89 service became number 7 in 1965 when it was extended across the city centre to Thornton. In 1967 the terminal arrangements were altered to include an anti-clockwise loop via the former Bradford Moor terminal stop, returning to Leeds Road via Hawthorn Street. Karrier 687, one of those rebuilt after the war by Samlesbury Engineering (including the addition of sliding windows to both decks) is seen turning at the terminus during a special trip for local transport photographers in June 1961. This was its very first appearance following painting in the pre-war dark blue livery for the Trolleybus Jubilee. (J.S.King)

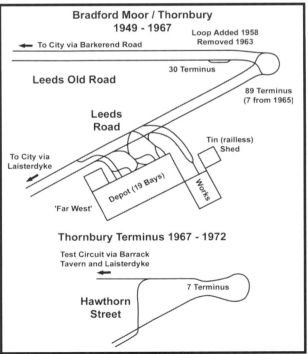

61.   The mainstay of the Thornbury route in its early days was the Crossley rebodied AEC and Karrier vehicles as shown by AEC/Crossley 652 passing Thornbury depot, en route to City, in September 1958. On the left, Bradford's last tram (car 104), then newly restored, can be seen during one of its periodic Saturday afternoon outings up and down the works yard. This operation was possible using the trolleybus positive wiring and the extant tram rails. Increasing technical difficulties forced the cessation of these rides in the mid 1960s, and tram 104 now resides in the Bradford Industrial Museum together with Karrier trolleybus 737. (A.D.Packer/J.Copland)

WIBSEY & BUTTERSHAW

62. Trolleybuses reached Wibsey in April 1955, replacing motorbuses, although a peak-hour electric service had operated as far as the foot of St Enoch's Road at Little Horton since the previous November (see photograph 66). This is the Wibsey terminus of service 45 in May 1957. The vehicles turned in the wide High Street at Acre Lane. Karrier E4 689, one of those rebuilt by Samlesbury, stands at the terminus. (A.D.Packer/J.Copland)

63. In April 1956, a branch off the Wibsey route of just over a mile in length was opened. Given service number 46, it diverged at St Enoch's Road Top into the Buttershaw housing estate along Reevy Road West to its junction with Cooper Lane. Rebodied AEC 654 makes the turn at the roundabout which formed the Buttershaw terminus. (R.F.Mack)

ST. ENOCH'S ROAD TOP

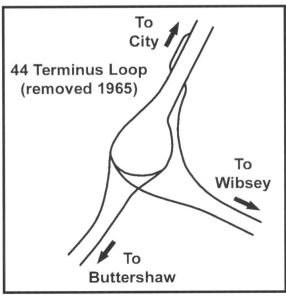

To
City

**44 Terminus Loop
(removed 1965)**

To
Wibsey

To
Buttershaw

64.   St Enoch's Road Top was the junction of the Wibsey and Buttershaw routes and vehicles could turn short here. From 1957 this was the terminus of the cross-city service 44 to Eccleshill. Trolleybuses showed 44 towards here and 33 when operating to Eccleshill. A loop was provided to allow these workings to wait clear of Wibsey/Buttershaw vehicles. The through service to Eccleshill was withdrawn in November 1962, and shortly before this, Doncaster BUT 834 with almost brand new East Lancs body waits to return across Bradford to Eccleshill. These trolleybuses entered service in July and August 1962. On the left of this shot, one of Bradford's ex London Transport RT motorbuses can be seen at the end of Moore Avenue. (S.Lockwood coll.)

65. The battle of the Regents. These vehicles are making the long ascent of St Enoch's Road from Little Horton in July 1968. The overtaking trolleybus is Doncaster 833 with a BUT 9611T chassis, which was the electric version of the AEC Regent III motorbus. The motorbus seen here is one of Bradford AEC Regent Vs with lightweight Metro-Cammell bodies which compared unfavourably both in comfort and performance with the trolleybus beside it. (A.D.Packer/J.Copland)

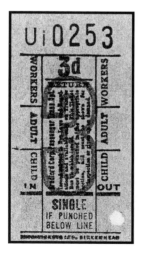

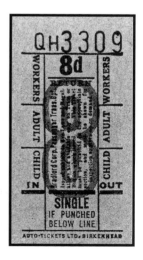

Notice No. 3073
30th December, 1969

NOTICE TO TROLLEYBUS DRIVERS
TROLLEYBUSES BECOMING 'ALIVE'

The attention of trolleybus drivers is drawn to rule 25(a) of Rules & Regulations 1958, which details the procedure to be adopted when a trolleybus in service becomes 'alive'.

Trolleybus drivers must ensure that in such cases, when there is a risk of passengers receiving an electric shock, the trolley booms are pulled down before passengers are allowed to alight. Such passengers should be transferred on to the following vehicle and the Inspector notified by the quickest means possible.

Drivers are at the same time reminded that the danger of electric shock is greatly diminished by use of the handbrake whenever a trolleybus is at rest and disciplinary action will be taken in all cases of a trolleybus being held on the footbrake.

E.Deakin
General Manager

66. At the foot of St Enoch's Road was a turning circle designated Little Horton. Although the wiring on the complete route to Wibsey was available by late 1954, initially the power supply arrangements were not sufficient to support a full service. From November of that year a tea time peak hour service of trolleybuses began, supplementing the motorbuses, but operating to the Little Horton circle only. This was the bleak scene at Little Horton in February 1955 showing utility Karrier 719 on this working. Note the vehicle is showing 'Duplicate Bus' rather than service 47, which later applied to this turning point. It was in damp, icy conditions such as this that a trolleybus could sometimes become 'alive' through the build up of slush on its underside, giving the unwary passenger a slight shock. In such a circumstance the vehicle would be taken out of service immediately. (A.D.Packer/J.Copland)

67. In May 1957, a spur route, a third of a mile long, was opened from Little Horton Lane along Horton Park Avenue to a turning circle at the County Cricket Ground and Bradford AFC football ground. As well as serving the sports facility, it also provided a turning place for specials to St Luke's Hospital on Little Horton Lane. These wires were also used on Armistice Sunday, when Victoria Square in the city centre was closed to traffic, and Little Horton Lane trolleybuses were required to fly-shunt into and out of Horton Park Avenue. This view shows the wiring junction in Little Horton Lane

looking towards Wibsey. It was a typical Bradford overhead installation of the time, using an interlaced turnout to save space and weight of fittings. Approaching from St Enoch's Road Top is a Llanelly Karrier on the through service to Eccleshill and behind that is a Yorkshire Woollen District Guy motorbus heading for Chester Street bus station. (R.Marshall)

68. This is a view of Horton Park Avenue in June 1957, a few weeks after the spur opened, with Notts and Derby AEC 580 unloading sports fans at the ground. Newer trolleybuses were able to show 'Sports Ground' when operating to here. Situated on a former tram route, the wiring was supported on existing tramway traction poles. The wires were dismantled in 1969 after a short period of disuse and two years before the remainder of the Little Horton Lane services. Behind the wall on the far side of the road is the Great Northern Halifax/ Keighley railway, which later crossed the Clayton trolleybus route as seen in photograph 18. (A.D.Packer/J.Copland)

69.   The Manningham Lane services entered the city centre at Forster Square via the descent of Manor Row and Cheapside. At the junction of Manningham Lane and Manor Row, with Busby's store in the left background, is utility Jo'burg 699. The wires branching off to the left of this view form the emergency link via North Parade, Rawson Square and John Street to Westgate on the Duckworth Lane route. The pull handle to access these wires is on the traction pole immediately to the right of the vehicle and the instruction 'Pull for North Parade' can be seen painted in a dark square on the pole. There was also provision for vehicles to turn back to Manor Row from Rawson Square, a facility which was used in June and July 1950 following the Forster Square fire. This is another of Bob Mack's photographs showing a coincidence in registration numbers (see photograph 14). This one shows the numerical extremes – from no 1 on the Hillman Minx car on the left to no 999 on the trolleybus. This view dates from around 1949/1950. (J.Fozard/R.F.Mack)

70. The rarely used North Parade wiring was a popular choice to be included on enthusiasts tours of the system and the entry into service of the Darlington single decker T403 in 1957 provided an unusual vehicle to use on these trips. Here the vehicle is seen in North Parade looking towards Rawson Square on 17th February. At Rawson Square (where the West Yorkshire Bristol bus is seen) the wires diverged right via John Street to Westgate or left back into Manor Row. (J.Fozard/R.F.Mack)

71. This is Forster Square during the Second World War, showing the terminal stand for the Manningham Lane services beside the stub terminus for the Bradford Moor trams. Behind the Square is the Post Office and, at higher level, stands Bradford Cathedral with Church Bank to the right. This is almost certainly a Bank Holiday scene, when all available trolleybuses from other depots were drafted in to supplement the service, moving the crowds to the delights of Lister Park or Shipley Glen near Saltaire. The lead trolleybus here is Duckworth Lane AEC 614 with original English Electric body in ultramarine livery, a vehicle that would normally never be seen operating to Saltaire. The number screen shows a very incorrect '7'. (A.D.Packer coll.)

72. Following the abandonment of the Bradford Moor trams in 1949, Forster Square was re-modelled and a gyratory routeing was adopted around an enlarged central garden area. At the beginning of 1950, this enabled the resumption of through services between Bradford Moor and the Manningham Lane routes, a feature of the pre-war tram service. A lower level view taken around 1960 shows AEC 603 with post-war Northern Coach builders body (soon to be painted in Trolleybus Jubilee livery) departing for Crossflatts. Note the three lines of wiring. The outer wires loop around the Square, the middle wires proceed towards Cheapside and Manningham Lane, whilst the inner set turns into Broadway. Also noteworthy is the small grilled economy version of the trend setting Ford Anglia car overtaking 603. (R.F.Mack)

CROSSFLATTS AND BRADFORD MOOR
30, 24 and 25

Bradford Moor (1)
2   Killinghall Road (2)
2 2 Hanson School (3)
3 2 2 Harris Street (4)
4 3 2 2 City (5)
4 4 3 2 2 Hallfield Road (6)

73.   The redevelopment of the Forster Square area in 1962 resulted in the removal of trolleybuses from this area. The Bradford Moor service was converted to motorbuses, whilst the Manningham Lane services survived almost a further year until October 1963 using a temporary turning circle at the foot of Cheapside outside the Midland Hotel. There were two versions of this as redevelopment work progressed, the second being of tighter radius than the first. The latter version of the circle is shown here, with Cheapside ascending on the left. Departing for Saltaire is Notts and Derby 590 rebodied by East Lancs in 1958. This view shows clearly the effect of an 8 feet wide body on a 7 feet 6 inches wide chassis, resulting in the overhang of the body over the rear wheel arch, only the front axle being lengthened to 8 feet when these vehicles were rebodied. The position of the side destination indicator, nearer the centre of the vehicle than normal, indicates that 590 was fitted with a sliding platform door, albeit rarely used. Behind 590 is Mexborough Sunbeam 847, which in March 1963 was the last Bradford trolleybus to enter service. During the severe winter of 1962/3, there had been a loss of traffic to better equipped West Yorkshire buses and to stem this the Roe and Weymann bodied BUTs at Saltaire Depot had been replaced with trolleybuses having more modern passenger facilities (chiefly heaters and doors). (R.F.Mack)

74.   The strategic direct link between Forster Square and Town Hall Square via Broadway was wired for trolleybuses in 1953. The intention was to operate a through service from Eccleshill via Forster Square through to Victoria Square. Difficulties with terminating a service at Victoria Square meant that plans were put on hold. The first trolleybus to use the Broadway link was Notts and Derby 588, still in that operator's dark blue livery, on the annual enthusiasts tour held on 20th June 1954. Shown here is the distinctive rear of the Weymann bodied vehicle as it stands at the Forster Square end of Broadway. This wiring eventually came into service use in November 1957 upon the introduction of the through service 44 between Eccleshill and St Enoch's Road Top. (C.W.Routh)

75.   The Leeds Road route from Thornbury terminated at Hall Ings, turning via Leeds Road and Bridge Street. At the terminal stop there was a large concrete waiting shelter that had existed since tramway days. This was referred to locally as 'Tut's Tomb' (a reference to King Tutankhamen). The shelter included an integral shop and there were large glass panels showing the route 89 and Thornbury. Pre-war AEC 606 with wartime utility Brush body is seen leaving the Hall Ings for Thornbury, passing under the inbound wires. On the right is the Ritz cinema at the junction with Broadway. City centre reconstruction in 1964 resulted in the Thornbury service using a temporary turning circle outside the cinema. In 1965 the service was routed via an extended Hall Ings behind the Town Hall through to Town Hall Square and Thornton, returning to Leeds Road via Market Street and Bank Street. (J.S.King)

76.   This is the bottom of Leeds Road, outside Exchange Station, on Tuesday 2nd July 1968. In mid-morning, Bradford, along with many other areas east of the Pennines, suffered a terrific rainstorm with almost an inch of rain falling in a few minutes. The effect on the city centre was catastrophic, with most roads becoming instant rivers. The pedestrian subways in Forster Square were flooded to the roof. Karrier 703, on the through service to Thornton, is seen caught in the chaos shortly after the storm.(Telegraph and Argus)

77.   The Wakefield Road services were routed in the city centre via a one-way loop, terminating in Union Street opposite St George's Hall, Bradford's principal concert venue. From Union Street, the loop proceeded back to Wakefield Road via Nelson Street and Croft Street. This is Union Street on 1st March 1952 showing Karrier E4 683 on service to Dudley Hill and AEC 643 overtaking en route to Tong Cemetery. There were loops in the overhead to allow such a manoeuvre.
(A.D.Packer/J.Copland)

78.   In 1963, Hall Ings was extended across Bridge Street to run behind the Town Hall. The terminus for the Wakefield Road services was then moved from Union Street into the new section of Hall Ings. The following year additional wiring was erected along here leading from the original Hall Ings to create a connection to Town Hall Square via Town Hall Street, the link being used by depot workings and from 1965 by the Thornbury to Thornton through service. This view of the new arrangement shows Union Street in the background on the site where the Norfolk Gardens Hotel would be built, and the vacant ground beside Hall Ings which was used for a time as a terminus for motorbus services. The vehicles shown are Doncaster BUT 835 loading for Holme Wood and alongside this, on the Wakefield service, is a West Riding Guy Wulfrunian bus (originally owned by Lancashire United and the only Wulfrunian with a Northern Counties body). (Photobus)

79.   On its way back to Wakefield Road, Notts and Derby BUT 762 is in Nelson Street passing the terminus of the no 64 Huddersfield bus service, operated jointly between the two Corporations and Hebble Motor Services. The motorbus is an AEC Regent V and was the last rear entrance bus purchased by Huddersfield Corporation. In the background is a Samuel Ledgard Leyland bus. Until 1940, the Oakenshaw trolleybus service operated from the city centre past this location, but there was no connection in the wiring with that of the Wakefield Road trolleybuses. (J.S.King)

80.   When the Clayton trolleybus service was opened in 1926, the vehicles turned in the city centre from Thornton Road via New Victoria Street and Victoria Square to the terminal stop at the very end of Thornton Road, beside the New Inn. The Thornton trolleybuses, introduced in late 1934, followed this same routeing but the City terminus was opposite the Alhambra Theatre at Victoria Square and a loop was provided to allow Clayton trolleybuses to pass. This is a view of Victoria Square showing the Thornton loop in the background. AEC 611, almost brand new, is seen in the foreground with another of the same type also in view. Stanley King's research has established that the 1934/5 season pantomime at the Alhambra was 'Red Riding Hood' thus proving that his photograph dates from shortly after the opening of the Thornton service. From 1942 the Thornton terminus was moved to the New Victoria cinema (later the Gaumont) in Thornton Road and the loop was removed. Ten years later the Clayton and Thornton services ceased to use these wires altogether, and commenced to turn round using Town Hall Square. (British Commercial Vehicle Museum/AEC)

81.   The conversion of the Wibsey route to trolleybuses in 1954/5 brought wiring back to the Victoria Square area. A turning circle was erected around the Square itself, which was accessible from either the City or Wibsey directions. This is the bottom of Little Horton Lane with a smart looking utility Karrier 738 starting the ascent on a peak-hour extra working to Little Horton, showing the wiring connections from Victoria Square on the left. Note the art deco frontage of the Bradford Camera Exchange just in front of the vehicle. (J.Fozard)

82.   By the late 1960s the city centre redevelopment was concentrated on the Town Hall Square area, which had by then been renamed The Tyrls. The Clayton and Thornton terminal stops were moved to here in early 1970. Access to Little Horton Lane was via a new dual carriageway named Princes Way, alongside the Gaumont cinema and on the approximate site of the former New Victoria Street. This was the last public roadway in Britain to be wired for trolleybuses. Karrier 717, one of the ten of this type rebodied with a rear entrance East Lancs body in 1957, is passing Victoria Square in October 1969. A similar vehicle can be seen in the distance turning from Thornton Road onto the new wiring in Princes Way. Also in view is the Provincial Building Society building under construction at the end of Thornton Road. This was demolished in 2002. (S.Lockwood)

83.   A scene in Town Hall Square as it was in the 1950s and 1960s with its subterranean toilets and overshadowed by the Town Hall (renamed City Hall in 1965). AEC 622 with post war Northern Coachbuilders body is seen turning here before commencing a journey to Pasture Lane. The inner set of wiring gave access to Little Horton Lane for Wibsey and Buttershaw workings. Between 1964 and 1968 wires emerged from Town Hall Street (in the right background) which were used by the cross-city Thornbury to Thornton trolleybuses and vehicles entering service from Thornbury Depot. (J.S.King)

84. This is the end of Thornton Road looking towards Town Hall Square. The Clayton services stood near the New Inn (just visible in the right background) with the Thornton service waiting outside the Gaumont cinema (behind the camera). The wiring allowed for both services to have unimpeded access to these stands. Two second–hand vehicles are seen, Darlington 790 overtaking St Helens 801 at the Pasture Lane stop. The buildings to the left (including the former Tatler cinema) were demolished in the late 1960s to make way for the Provincial Building Society headquarters. (J.S.King)

85. Tyrrel Street was the city centre terminus for the Wibsey, Buttershaw and St Enoch's Road services. There was also through wiring to allow trolleybuses entering service from Duckworth Lane depot to access the Thornton route at Thornton Road. This busy scene, taken about 1960, shows Hastings 815, one of a pair with Weymann bodies, loading for Buttershaw with a Darlington close up behind. The Hastings vehicle is in the short-lived experimental livery with less cream. Collinson's Café was on the opposite side of the street. (Travel Lens Photographic)

86.   At the other end of Tyrrel Street, by the junction with Sunbridge Road, was the turning circle for the Duckworth Lane and Allerton services. There were four sets of wires in Sunbridge Road, two for each direction as far as Godwin Street, where the Duckworth Lane service diverged. This allowed unimpeded access to both terminal stops, which was vital in the case of the Duckworth Lane trolleybuses with departures every two minutes at peak times. This early post-war elevated view of Sunbridge Road shows AEC/Northern Coachbuilders 611 loading for Duckworth Lane. A similar vehicle on the Allerton route descends the hill towards the turning circle just off to the right. The crossover in the wiring (bottom right) allowed vehicles from Duckworth Lane depot to access the Allerton wires. This was moved into the turning circle at a later date and there was a corresponding crossover for vehicles working back to the depot from the Allerton route. Note both the distinctive shape of rear emergency door on 611, which was derived from the London trolleybus bodies that Northern Coachbuilders built during the war, and the rear destination display that was reduced to a number display from the mid 1950's. (Walter Scott (Bradford) Ltd.)

87.   The Duckworth Lane service entered the city centre via Westgate and Godwin Street and Notts and Derby AEC 587 can be seen at the junction of these streets during the mid-1950s. In 1969 the outward route of Duckworth Lane trolleybuses was diverted via Barry Street instead of Godwin Street due to the introduction of a one-way traffic scheme. 587 was one of the first Notts and Derby AECs to enter service in 1953, having been painted in Bradford livery before leaving its original owners. (R.F.Mack)

DRIVER TRAINING

88.   Bradford had extensive facilities for trolleybus driver training. As well as the use of former passenger vehicles numbered in the ancillary fleet, there was also an off-road training ground. This was situated at the former Bowling Hill tramway permanent way yard off Wakefield Road, between Dudley Hill and the city centre and adjacent to the Bowling motorbus depot. In 1956 an unconnected spur of wiring was erected from Wakefield Road into the yard with a circle of wires within. From 1962 the layout was extended to include a triangular reverser. When the Wakefield Road trolleybus service was closed in April 1967, the training ground continued in operation, and access was achieved by the training vehicle (at this time BUT 060, ex 745) using the otherwise redundant Wakefield Road wires for its daily trip to and from Thornbury depot. Eventually, in late 1967, wiring demolition meant that 060 had to be kept at Bowling Hill permanently until the facility was closed in February 1968. This view, taken shortly after the closure of the Wakefield Road route, shows 060 working in the yard passing the reverser. Note the 'roadway' marked out using redundant concrete stop poles.(J.S.King)

89.   This photograph was taken during the last ever Ministry of Transport trolleybus driving test, which took place on Friday 30th July 1971. At the top of Whetley Hill on the Duckworth Lane route, the examinee is being given an unexpected extra opportunity to demonstrate his skills by having to coast past a stretch of wiring under emergency repair. For the record the final examinee was Mr G S Watson and the examiner, who issued the pass certificate on arrival at Sunbridge Road in the city centre, was Bradford City Transport's Chief Driving Examiner, Inspector Gobbi. The vehicle is BUT 063, formerly no 746 in its passenger service. It was withdrawn from service immediately after the test but was purchased for preservation and is now restored to working order as no 746 at the Trolleybus Museum at Sandtoft. (S.Lockwood)

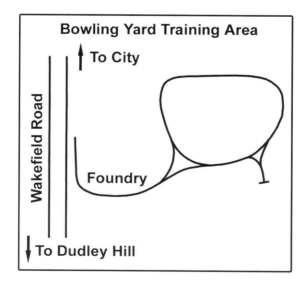

DEPOTS AND WORKS

90.   Throughout the trolleybus era, Bradford's policy was to maintain several small depots at the outer ends of routes. The largest of these was at Leeds Road, Thornbury, where the overhaul works was also located. The depot and works was established in 1900, and expanded over the following ten years, resulting in three running sheds. The works access was by way of a long approach road alongside the depot building. Adjacent to this access road, a shed was erected in 1915 to house the railless fleet, and this continued as a running shed until 1930, by which time the main depot was being used for trolleybuses. Known as the 'tin' or 'railless' shed, it survived as a store for trolleybuses waiting for rebodying or latterly for withdrawn vehicles awaiting disposal. Between 1964 and 1968, very few surplus trolleybuses were sold, resulting in this shed, and the 'Far West' area of the main depot, being filled with such vehicles. The works approach road, with the 1915 'railless' shed on the left, is seen here in 1968. Note the 'Car Depot and Workshops' inscription over the works entrance. The two BUT trolleybuses, 744 and 748, have been in storage since early 1964 and have been brought out to prepare for disposal as scrap. (J.S.King)

91.   This glimpse inside Thornbury depot was no doubt taken to show a new gadget for the interior cleaning of vehicles. It is, however, the only known view of 'Queenie', the AEC Q trolleybus 633 in its Bradford livery. (BCT/J.S.King coll.)

92.   This is the other end of the Depot from the works, showing no 3 shed. Behind the administration block on the right is the 'Far West', where surplus trolleybuses were stored in the last years of the system. This photograph was taken during an enthusiasts tour on 13th September 1959 and shows, on the right, Karrier 730 with its brand new front entrance East Lancs body, having just re-entered service. On the left is 736, one of the same batch of vehicle, but still with its utility Roe body. A few days later, it too would be withdrawn for rebodying. The front entrance DKY vehicles were one of the few trolleybus types that were never permanently allocated to Thornbury, their entire life in this form being spent operating from Duckworth Lane depot. Thornbury depot had an exclusive trolleybus allocation from 1952 until 1962, when the Bradford Moor trolleybuses gave way to motorbuses, and the final trolleybus allocation was for the Clayton route which closed at the end of July, 1971. (C.W.Routh)

93.   Just below Bolton Junction on Bolton Road, was situated Bolton depot which was Bradford's first electric tram depot when it opened in 1898. It housed trolleybuses from 1930 and became exclusively trolleybus from 1934 on conversion of the Eccleshill tram route. There were four roads plus a siding wire outside the southern facing wall. Initially six-wheel double deckers were allocated, with single deckers for the Eccleshill service. Just before the war the Karrier E4s of the 677-692 batch were introduced here. The last allocation seems to have been the Karrier/Roe utility vehicles numbered between 703 and 714. In later years the depot was effectively a sub–shed of Thornbury. Difficulties in accommodating eight feet wide trolleybuses and the dangers of reversing out into an increasingly busy Bolton Road prompted the depot's closure on 2nd November 1958, with Thornbury taking over its work. This view of the depot, just before closure, shows utility Karrier 703 in the siding. (J.S.King)

94.   Duckworth Lane depot was situated on the road of that name and at the original terminus of the route. Inside, there were eight roads and access was to and from the city direction only, all vehicles having to reverse out. From 1935 the depot operated trolleybuses exclusively until November 1971, when some motorbuses were allocated. The routes operated were: Allerton, Duckworth Lane and Thornton. Until 1960, the depot ran AEC vehicles (but only three of the CAK batch) plus a brief time with rebodied Jo'burgs and Darlingtons. From May 1960 with the allocation of the DKY front entrance Karriers it was Britain's only depot to operate exclusively front entrance trolleybuses. It never ran BUT vehicles, except for a few weeks when 835 was allocated there. Following the conversion of the Allerton service in February 1971, the depot assumed responsibility for the Wibsey/Buttershaw services from Thornbury depot until these routes closed in July of that year. This view dates from 1966. (J.S.King)

OTHER DEPOTS

SALTAIRE

The depot at Saltaire dated from 1904 and trolleybuses replaced trams here upon conversion of the Crossflatts service in 1939. This was the only service operated from the depot, the Saltaire via Thackley trolleybuses always being the responsibility of Bolton depot or later Thornbury. The six road facility continued until the end of the Crossflatts trolleybus service in late 1963, although a loop of wiring was retained for emergency use by Thackley trolleybuses until their demise in June 1971. Saltaire's allocation was initially from the CAK batch of AEC vehicles. After the war the eight feet wide BUT trolleybuses came here. During the last year of trolleybuses, more modern types such as rebodied Notts & Derby AECs, Darlington and Mexborough vehicles were allocated to compare more favourably with 'West Yorkshire' buses. (See photo 51.)

BANKFOOT

Situated on Manchester Road, this tram depot housed railless vehicles for the Oakenshaw service from 1914 until the route's demise in 1940. One road was wired for these vehicles and only four were allocated here, even after the service was extended into the city centre. Initially these were taken from the 503–520 batch of railless single deckers, but after the late 1920's Leyland/English Electric vehicles were used. Double deck trolleybuses were never operated. Although the terminus of the route to Bolton was just across the road, there was never any involvement with this service. Bankfoot became Bradford's final tram depot and the last tram (no 104) ran into here on 6th May 1950.

ROLLING STOCK

95. 240–241(502–501)   AK8090, AK4516
    503-520   AK9621-37,9639 (not consecutively)
    523–528   KU 1161–1166

These vehicles comprised the original railless fleet, all entering service between 1911 and 1922.

240 and 241 were the initial vehicles and, until 1913, were numbered in the tram series, after which a railless series was commenced, starting at 501. 241 became 501, 240 becoming 502. They were supplied to Bradford by the Railless Electric Traction Company and had Hurst Nelson 28 seat open rear platform bodies on Alldays and Onions chassis. Both were converted into trolley/battery lorries in 1916 (502) and 1918 (501) and they ran as such until withdrawal in 1926 (see photograph 3). It is reputed that the cabs of these vehicles were subsequently incorporated into the Corporation's tram works car no 11.

503 to 520 were a production batch with 29 seats used to expand the system and were built by the Corporation at Thornbury Car Works using David Brown chassis components. They were given registration numbers in 1921 and were withdrawn between 1923 and 1929. The last of all to survive was 514 which served as a driver training bus between 1928 and 1930.

523 to 528 were built by the Corporation in late 1922/early 1923, using AEC chassis parts. They were front

entrance 30 seat vehicles for operation by one man, had saloon doors, folding steps, and a distinctive livery of teak with a white roof. From 1926 they were fitted with pneumatic tyres and were withdrawn in 1930/31 (see photograph 5).

Seen in Thornbury works yard in 1929 is 511, one of the last of the 1914 raillesses to survive, and probably just withdrawn. Alongside it, by comparison is ADC 541, new in 1927 and one of the type with the front axle behind the entrance (for details see photograph 98). (R.Marshall coll.)

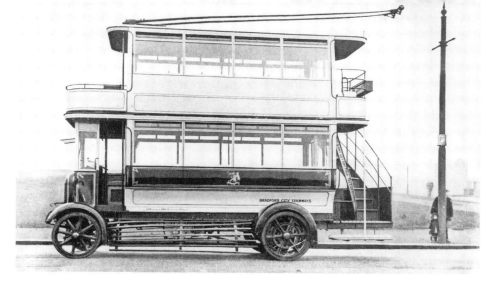

96.   **521 AK 9638**

Built in 1920, this was the world's first covered top double deck trolleybus and was immediately dubbed the 'flying cottage loaf'. It was built in the Corporation's tramway workshops at Thornbury using Kirkstall Forge components. The 51 seat open staircase body had the resistances housed in the open front balcony. It ran until October 1928. This photograph shows the brand new vehicle and was taken in Killinghall Road. Through the cab window can be seen the tram type hand controller which the driver had to operate as well as the steering. The low speed of operation ensured that this was possible – 521 had a top speed of 18 miles per hour. The man and child waiting at the stop on the opposite side of the road must be wondering what sort of contraption was coming their way.(BCT/S.Lockwood coll.)

97.   **522 AK 9963**

This vehicle was a development of the previous double deck design and incorporated twin-steering axles at the front. It had 59 seats to a similar open balcony design to 521. Constructed at Thornbury Works using Kirkstall Forge parts it was the first trolleybus with a foot controller and had a top speed of 19 miles per hour. The open rear staircase was later enclosed. It was withdrawn in January 1927 and the body was used as a store in Thornbury tram depot until 1930. This unlikely looking machine is seen in Killinghall Road on the Bolton–Bankfoot service. The large window bill in the lower saloon advertises the 'Arctic Fur Company - half shop prices'. (BCT/S.Lockwood coll.)

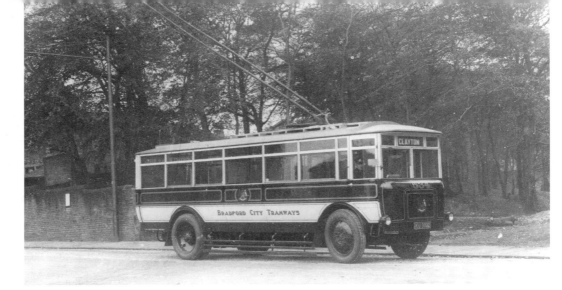

98.　　**529-543　KU 9104–6, KU 9101–3, RT 1345, UM 1755, KW 204–6, KW 200–203**

A mixed bag of single deckers was delivered in 1926/7 chiefly for the Clayton route and to replace some of the original railless fleet. Significantly they were the first vehicles in the fleet fitted from new with pneumatic, rather than solid tyres. Vehicle details were :-

529-531 ADC 607 with Strachan 31 seat centre entrance body.
532-535, 537-539 Garratt '0' with Roe 31 seat centre entrance body.
536 Garrett 'S' with Roe 31 seat centre entrance body.
540-543 ADC 603 with Strachan front entrance body. 540 had 37 seats and the others 30 seats.

The entrance door was ahead of the front axle making this quartet of vehicles suitable for one-man operation (see photograph 95).

The ADCs were essentially AEC chassis marketed under the Associated Daimler Company name, and were the only trolleybuses so designated. They were withdrawn in 1937/8.

Garretts 535 and 536 had previously been demonstrators hence their non-Bradford registration numbers. 536 was the first ever Garratt trolleybus and had previously been tried in Leeds and Keighley. It ran in Bradford in its original red livery, being inevitably dubbed 'the fire engine'. 535 had previously operated in Leeds, Ipswich and Mexborough. Although 536 was withdrawn in 1931, the remaining Garretts survived until 1935/6.

Garrett 534 is seen when new at Clayton in 1926. (BCT/R.Marshall coll.)

Bradford City Transport

Final Trolleybus Operation in Great Britain

Sunday, 26th March, 1972

Departing from the Odeon Cinema

Thornton Road at **11 30**

Duration of Tour approximately 2 hours
Time allowed at certain points for photographs

Fare £1.00　　**Tour No.** **6**

99. 544-560 KW 2601-2610, 4600 – 4605, CK 3898

Although ordered from English Electric, these 36 seat centre entrance single deckers were sub contracted to Leyland Motors to build. The chassis were of Leyland PLTB1 type based on the successful 'Lion' motorbus. 560 had been a Leyland demonstrator in Ashton under Lyne and Maidstone. The vehicles entered service in 1928/1929 and lasted until 1938/1940. They were used principally on the Clayton route (before it was converted to take double deckers) and also the Oakenshaw service, for which some were based at

Bankfoot tram depot. The first ten (544-553) had a more rounded front to the Leyland bodywork.

This view shows 554, on test when brand new, passing the Barrack Tavern on Killinghall Road. A large print of this photograph hung for many years in the Chief Inspector's office at the Forster Square headquarters of Bradford City Transport.(BCT/J.S.King coll.)

100. 561–596 KW 6051–67, KW 6654–6659, KW 9453–9464, KY 1360

This group of trolleybuses, built entirely by English Electric, was delivered between late 1929 and early 1932. There were four variations :-
561–571 34 seat front entrance two axle single deck.
572–583 56 seat three axle double deck flat fronted.
584–595 56 seat three axle double deck round fronted
596 Three axle double deck (ex English Electric demonstrator)
The 11 single deckers lasted until the latter end of the war, eking out their existence on the Eccleshill service and on peak hour extras. The 25 double deckers were the first bulk purchase of this type in the fleet and were bought for the first tram conversions on the Allerton, Saltaire via Thackley, and Greengates routes. No more three axle

vehicles were purchased after these deliveries. They had a varied life. 588 was scrapped as early as 1934 following extensive accident damage. Of the remainder, ten were sold to Newcastle Corporation where some were put into service, running until 1946. and a further three went to nearby South Shields Corporation in 1945. The remainder were withdrawn by April 1946. This posed shot in Killinghall Road shows flat fronted double deck 582 together with single deck 572.
(BCT/S.Lockwood coll.)

101.   633   KY 6210

This trolleybus was thirty years ahead of its time and Bradfordians marvelled when they first set eyes on it. It was the electric version of the AEC side engined 'Q' motorbus (of which Bradford also had an example). Only five of these trolleybuses were ever built and three went for export to Sydney Australia. The other joined the Southend fleet. Bradford's was numerically the first, chassis no 761T001, and it arrived in February 1934 as a demonstrator in cream livery with light green bands. The body seated 63 passengers, which was a very high capacity for a two axle vehicle at that time. Bought by the Corporation in September 1934 and given the fleet number 633, it eventually gained standard Bradford livery (see photograph 91). The front entrance and single rear wheels set right at the back made this double decker unique in the fleet and the latter feature proved troublesome in icy weather when the vehicle was prone to lose its grip on the road. Lasting until the end of 1941, it was sold to South Shields Corporation who ran it until 1951. This photograph shows the vehicle in 'as built' condition at the maker's works. Before entry into service in Bradford the exterior handrails by the front door were removed and the trolley gantry was fitted with shrouds on each side. Platform doors, absent at first, were fitted later. (R.Marshall coll.)

→

102.   597 – 632   KY 8200 – 8220
AAK 420 – 434

The Thornton and Duckworth Lane trams were replaced by this batch of 36 AEC 661T trolleybuses with English Electric metal framed bodywork. They entered service in two groups, 597 to 617 in the last months of 1934 and the remainder in the latter half of 1935. Apart from 633, these were the first 'modern' trolleybuses in Bradford and had streamlined styling like contemporary motorbuses rather than looking like converted tramcars. Other features were regenerative braking and nos 597 – 617 had a half cab arrangement with an inward facing double seat beside the driver. Structural problems resulted in a normal full width cab being installed by 1937. All were rebodied, nine by Brush during the war and the remainder by Northern Coachbuilders between 1947 and 1949. (See photographs 106 & 108). Brand new 601 is seen before entering service. The handrail for the additional seat facing the driver can be seen at the nearside front of the vehicle. (S.Lockwood collection)

103.   **634- 676   BAK 934   CAK 635 – 676**
        This large batch of trolleybuses, delivered between 1937 and 1939, enabled the tram conversions on Wakefield Road and Manningham Lane to be carried out. They were AEC 661T vehicles with English Electric lightweight metal framed bodywork. 634 was the prototype for the design and entered service in 1937 as a demonstrator, being exhibited at the Commercial Motor Show of that year. It was absorbed into the fleet in November. It could be distinguished from the others by the protruding destination boxes (see photograph 7). 635, the prototype of the production version, entered service during 1938 and the rest followed in late 1938 and 1939. After the war 637 was experimentally fitted with automatic acceleration equipment for a few years. Several of the batch were rebodied, five by Crossley in 1952, 10 by East Lancs in 1956, and a further vehicle (639) was given a second-hand Northern Coachbuilders body from 618. Withdrawals of those not rebodied commenced with 641 at the end of 1955, and the last survivors were 668 and 669 which ran until the end of 1959.
        645 is seen in Forster Square in 1950. Note the combined 'AEC/English Electric' badge on the front dash panel and the crew inspecting the devastation caused by the fire in June of that year.   (AB Cross)

104. **677 – 692   CAK 677 – 691**
                    DKU 692.

These 16 trolleybuses were on Karrier E4 chassis and had Weymann bodywork. 677 – 691 were placed in service in 1938/9. 692, built as a demonstrator, was the last Karrier E4 built, being offered to Bradford after the outbreak of war. It had detail differences to the rest of the batch, notably outswept skirt panels and the front route number was placed alongside the destination rather than above it. The suspension on these vehicles compared unfavourably with that on the preceding batch of AEC trolleybuses. Their early life was spent at Bolton Depot. In 1950, four (679,681,687 and 689) were given a thorough body rebuild by Samlesbury Engineering of Preston which resulted in these being fitted with sliding windows. Eight were given new Crossley bodies in 1952 (see photograph 110). Of the remainder, 683 was the first withdrawal in 1953. The quartet with rebuilt bodies lasted until 1961/2, with 687, which had been painted in its original ultramarine livery for the 1961 Trolleybus Jubilee, being the last survivor. This pre-war view shows 686, in original condition in dark blue livery, alongside the loading barriers at the foot of Bolton Road adjacent to the Transport Department head office. Note the 'Karrier/English Electric' badge on the front dash.(S.Lockwood coll.)

105. 693 – 702   DKW 993 – 999
DKY 2 – 4

In 1939, the South African Municipality of Johannesburg ordered 25 eight foot wide Sunbeam MF2 trolleybus chassis. Their delivery was prevented by the war and they were therefore allocated to British operators. Nottingham took five and the remaining 20 were shared equally between St Helens and Bradford. Delivered in 1942, Bradford's ten were fitted with utility Weymann bodies without side or rear destination apertures or even a rear emergency window. They were the first vehicles painted in the new lighter blue livery, which was inspired by similar shade carried by the four AEC trolleybuses borrowed from Southend on Sea earlier in the war. Special dispensation was needed to allow vehicles of this width to operate and they were initially restricted by the Ministry of Transport to the Saltaire/Crossflatts route operating out of Saltaire depot. The blank emergency doors were glazed shortly after the war and by 1951 the front destination arrangements had been altered to allow a route number to be displayed. All were withdrawn by 1953 and the chassis stored until 1955 when they were sent to East Lancashire Coachbuilders for rebodying (see photograph 11). Brand new 700 is seen on a test run at the Nab Wood turning circle between Saltaire and Bingley. (H.Brearley)

106. Brush rebodied AEC trolleybuses.

During the war, it became apparent that English Electric bodywork on the 1934/5 batch of AEC vehicles was in very poor state of repair. Permission was obtained to purchase new bodies for nine of these trolleybuses. They were built by Brush of Loughborough to their particularly ugly looking utility specification. The original seats and trolley gear (gantry and booms set at 18 inches spacing) were retained. The vehicles involved were 599, 600, 601, 605, 606, 608, 609, 612, 613.

599 overturned in Toller Lane in 1953 and was scrapped, but the rest lasted to the 1957-60 period. 601 is shown in its later life at the Eccleshill (Mechanics Institute) terminus. (J.S.King)

107.   **703-739**   DKY 703 – 739

37 Karrier W trolleybuses to Ministry of Supply utility specification were delivered to Bradford between 1945 and 1946. There were three batches as follows:

714-714	Roe bodies
715-733	Park Royal bodies
734-739	Roe bodies

The first batch of Roe bodies had wooden slatted seating until 1951. The rest were delivered with upholstered seats and the later Roe bodies were to a 'relaxed' utility style, visually more pleasing than the first batch. Ten of the Park Royal group were rebodied with East Lancashire rear entrance bodies between 1956 and 1958 and the remainder were given East Lancs front entrance bodies in 1959/60 (see photographs 112/3).

Roe bodied 712 is seen at Bolton Junction in October 1954. (A.B. Cross)

108.   **Northern Coachbuilders rebodied trolleybuses.**

The 27 remaining 1934/5 AEC vehicles were given new bodies by Northern Coachbuilders of Newcastle between 1946 and 1948. There were two types, the first batch of six having a severe frontal styling whilst the remainder had a more pleasing design. The vehicles affected were:

Type 1 (1946/7)	607,614,615,616,621,622
Type 2 (1947/8)	597/8/602/3/4/10/11/17/18/19/20/23-32.

The type 1 vehicles were the last trolleybuses to enter service fitted with trolley wheels. In 1955, 618 lost its body (the chassis was scrapped) which was transferred to 1938 AEC 639 (see photograph 28). Withdrawals took place between 1956 and 1962, making some of these vehicles amongst the longest lived Bradford trolleybus chassis. 603 was repainted in an interpretation of the 1911 livery for the Trolleybus Jubilee in 1961 and it achieved one million miles in service in April 1962, shortly before being withdrawn. 597 served as a permanent driver training vehicle (renumbered 060) between 1962 and 1964. This photograph shows 622 with its brand new type 1 body in Duckworth Lane. (J.A.Pitts)

109.   **740-759**   E K U
740 – 751, FKU 752 – 759.
These trolleybuses introduced the BUT 9611T chassis into the fleet, a type that was to become a firm favourite. However, this batch of twenty proved to be the last all-new trolleybuses that Bradford purchased. The first 12, for the new Bradford Moor route, came in 1949, followed by a final eight vehicles (intended to be used on the aborted Undercliffe route) in late 1950/early 1951. The bodywork was split between Roe (EKU) and Weymann (FKU) respectively. The Weymann vehicles in particular were extremely handsome. Early alterations were the fitment of automatic acceleration equipment and an increase in seating capacity from 56 to 59. Additionally 758 was fitted with flashing trafficators, the first passenger vehicle in the country to use such equipment. Withdrawals began in 1963 with 747, and all the remainder followed by March 1964. However, Bradford was reluctant to let such fine vehicles go and at the end of 1966 753, 757 and 758 returned to service, followed by 749 in March 1968. Additionally, three more had been returned to non-passenger use as driver training vehicles; 745 in 1964 (renumbered 060), and 743/746 in 1966 (062/063). 745 subsequently returned to passenger service in 1968. All these were withdrawn again in 1970-71, 063 performing the last Ministry of Transport driving test (see photograph 89) and 758, by then the last rear entrance trolleybus in service in the country, being withdrawn at the Clayton route closure in July 1971.

Weymann bodied 757 is seen at Crossflatts terminus in 1958, together with 746, one of the Roe bodied batch. (P.Watson/J.Copland)

110.   **Crossley rebodied trolleybuses**
        The next batch of vehicles to be rebodied were some 1938 AECs and 1939 Karrier E4s originally with English Electric or Weymann bodies. 13 vehicles were given new 59 seat bodies by Crossley Motors of Stockport. All re-entered service in March 1952. These bodies were the first in the fleet to incorporate twin track route number blinds The vehicles concerned were:

        AEC   635/6/7/640/652
        Karrier   677/8/682/4/5/8/691/2

        At first they were used on the new Thornbury trolleybus route 89, and 640 opened the service. They were withdrawn between November 1962 and October 1963. This photograph shows the lowest numbered vehicle of this type, AEC 635 in Forster Square. This vehicle was the first Bradford trolleybus to have matching fleet and registration numbers. (Photobus)

111.	760 – 774	NNU	224 – 238
	580 – 586	DRB	616 – 622
	587 – 596	HNU	826-830, 970-974

Bradford's first purchase of second-hand trolleybuses (other than demonstrators) was the acquisition of 32 vehicles from Notts & Derby Traction Company, whose trolleybus system was abandoned in April 1953. These vehicles, all Weymann bodied, comprised the entire operational fleet. The fifteen BUT 9611T trolleybuses (760-774) dated from 1949 so were still relatively new. The remainder were AEC vehicles dating from 1938 (DRB) or 1941 (HNU) and, not being modern vehicles, were numbered in a series first deployed on the English Electric six wheelers. The BUTs all entered service in 1953, many of them still in the Notts and Derby livery which was a similar, but darker blue to Bradford's own shade. 764 and 769 were given a special Coronation livery (see photograph 52). The AEC vehicles entered service gradually, between April 1953 and June 1955 starting with the HNUs. All the DRBs were withdrawn by 1958 having 'covered' for other trolleybuses sent away for rebodying, but the HNUs were deemed good enough to be rebodied themselves with East Lancashire bodies during 1958 (see next photograph). The BUTs lasted intact until July 1962 when 766 was withdrawn and the remainder followed until the last one (760) was taken out of service in January 1964. During their life they were fitted with automatic acceleration and several had their destination apertures altered to the Bradford pattern. 773 was used to experiment with trolley retrievers in 1956.

BUT 770 is seen in Union Street in the 1950s. This vehicle was subsequently purchased for preservation by the National Trolleybus Association and is currently awaiting restoration. (S.Lockwood coll.)

112. **Rebodied trolleybuses–East Lancashire rear entrance bodies.**

693 – 702   Jo'burgs (see photograph 105)
775 – 784   (CBX 530/531/600/601/909–914)
634,638,651,654,655,659,664,666,674,675 (see photograph 103)
715 – 720/722/723/724/727 (see photograph 107)
587 – 596   (see photograph 87)

    50 trolleybuses, of varying age and origins, were given new modern East Lancashire eight feet wide 63 seat bodies, re-entering service between January 1956 and June 1958. They were dealt with in five batches of ten vehicles corresponding to the listing above. Except for the Jo'burg vehicles, which were already eight feet wide, the chassis were all modified with a wider front axle. 775-784 were 1945-6 Karrier W trolleybuses which originated with Llanelly and District Traction Co and were bought by Bradford as chassis only in 1953, their utlilty bodies having been scrapped. All the other vehicles had run in Bradford before rebodying. All had provision for a rear sliding entrance door (with a corresponding built up rear with emergency door in the rear wall), although only 21, (701 and the last two batches), actually had the sliding doors fitted. The first four of the Llanelly trolleybuses had automatic acceleration equipment. Withdrawals commenced in 1964 with 591 although many of the Karriers lasted until June 1971. A trio of the Notts and Derby AECs (588,589 and 592) ran until July 1968 and became the last AEC trolleybuses to run in public service in Britain. The photograph shows Llanelly 784 within days of entering service in Bradford in February 1956 at the city centre terminus of the Duckworth Lane route. A Llanelly was a rare sight on this service and its presence here probably indicates that it was operating a weekend extra journey for hospital visitors. (A.D.Packer/J.S.King)

113. **Rebodied trolleybuses–East Lancashire Front entrance bodies.**

785 – 793 (GHN 403, 563,564,566,569,570,571,574,575)
703 – 714,721/5/6/8 - 739. (see photograph 107)

36 wartime Karrier W trolleybuses were fitted with East Lancs 8 feet wide front entrance bodies between December 1958 and August 1960, these being a development of the previous rear entrance design. The initial nine originated as single deckers with Darlington Corporation which had run with utility centre entrance Brush bodies in their home town. Apart from 785, (as T403-see photographs 9/30/70) none of the Darlingtons ran in Bradford service in single deck form and their greater wheelbase resulted in them being a foot longer (with 70 seats rather than 66) than the native vehicles in this group. Some were fitted with motors from the Hull 'Coronation' trolleybuses, and trolley retrievers were experimentally fitted to 788, 703, 705, 707, 711, 712 and 713 when newly rebodied. This group formed the mainstay of the last years of the system, the first to be withdrawn being 786 in July 1970, followed by 738 in November of that year after it had overturned at Thornton. The Darlingtons were all withdrawn by July 1971, and of the remainder, 703, 706, 711, 712, 713 and 735 lasted until the very end of the system. After withdrawal, 705 and 729 were destroyed by fire at Thornbury Depot in December 1971. This view shows the rear end profile of 705, the last of this type to enter service in August 1960, complete with trolley retrievers. The chrome rear bumpers were removed in the late 1960s.(J.S.King)

114.   **794 – 801   BDJ 82 – 89**
Origins: St. Helens Corporation. Built 1951. Bought by Bradford 1958.

These were BUT 9611T trolleybuses with East Lancashire bodies. They had the first chassis numbers for this type of vehicle (001 – 008). The bodies were renovated by Roe before entry into service which took place gradually during 1959. This included removal of the opening portion of the upper deck front windows, revised destination arrangements, rear emergency door alterations, and the addition of Bradford type embellishments on the front dash panel. On the chassis side, automatic acceleration was fitted. The first withdrawal took place in November 1965 with 797, although 795 and 799 lasted until July 1971, albeit with a period of storage in the mid-1960s. For second-hand vehicles that were not rebodied, this length of service is noteworthy. This view shows 796 in Leeds Road near Laisterdyke on a positioning journey from Thornbury Depot. (R.F.Mack)

115. 802-803
HUF 49-50
Origins:
Brighton Corporation.
Built 1948. Bought by
Bradford 1959

More BUT 9611T vehicles came in the form of this duo with Weymann bodies. For Bradford service they were given revised destination indicator arrangements and were up-seated to 59 from 56. They had coasting and run-back brake equipment but this was blanked off in Bradford service. 802 originally had an experimental livery with reduced cream relief. Neither vehicle lasted long, 803 being withdrawn in November 1962 and 802 in June 1963 following extensive accident damage. 802 is seen in this view turning into Broadway from Forster Square on the through service to St Enoch's Road Top. By the time this photograph was taken it had gained normal livery. (Photobus)

116.   804-815   BDY 804/805/796 – 803, 820/815
Origins: Hastings Tramways Company. Built 1946/7. Bought by Bradford 1959.

All but the last two of these Sunbeam W vehicles had Park Royal 56 seat bodies built almost to utility specification. 814/5 had Weymann 56 seat bodies. Apart from the provision of Bradford style destination indicator arrangements, these vehicles were not outwardly altered to any extent for Bradford service. They entered service in piecemeal fashion, from August 1959 (815) to May 1961 (809). Their life in Bradford was short – the final trio (810/811/814) being withdrawn in October 1963. 812 had the shortest life span, lasting just

23 months between January 1961 and November 1962. The power and brake pedals on these vehicles were on opposite sides to normal trolleybus practice and they entered service in Bradford still retaining this feature. The inevitable confusion for drivers resulted in the controls subsequently being altered. Park Royal bodied 806 is seen using the emergency turning loop at West Street in 1962. An example of a Weymann bodied ex-Hastings vehicle is seen in photograph 85. (A.D.Packer/J Copland)

117. **831 – 835   LHN 781 – 785**
      841 - 847   FWX 911 – 914, JWW 375 – 377
      Origins: 831–835: Darlington Corporation.

Built in 1949 with East Lancs rear entrance bodies, then bought by Doncaster Corporation in 1952. Acquired by Bradford in 1959. (A sixth member of the batch, LHN 780, was included but was scrapped for spares). These were the only third-hand trolleybuses in Britain.

841–847 : Mexborough and Swinton Traction Company. Built 1948 (FWX) or 1950 (JWW). Bodies : Brush single-deck centre entrance. Bought by Bradford in 1961 in chassis form only.

The final trolleybuses to enter service in Bradford were five BUT 9611T vehicles, (the 'Doncasters'), which appeared in July and August 1962, and seven Sunbeam F4 vehicles, (the 'Mexboroughs'), which took up service between December 1962 and March 1963. All twelve were rebodied before entering Bradford service with this updated style of 66 seat East Lancs body, the final development of the Bradford trolleybus. They were extremely handsome with extra deep windscreens and to a high specification. The BUT quintet had automatic acceleration equipment fitted, as well as fluorescent lighting. The Sunbeams, originally single-deckers, were one foot longer than the BUTs and had traction lighting. During the mid 1960s 835 was painted in an experimental darker blue. In the late 1960s 841/2/5/6 were fitted with two-way radio equipment. All these vehicles lasted until the final year of operation with the BUTs being withdrawn by the end of July 1971. 834 was the last trolleybus to operate to Clayton and 843, 844 and 845 played major roles in the final closure proceedings in March 1972, with 842 and 846 also being active right to the end.

Mexborough Sunbeam 847, Bradford's highest numbered trolleybus, departs from the city centre terminus at the end of Thornton Road en route to Pasture Lane. (Photobus)

BRADFORD TROLLEYBUSES
THAT NEVER WERE

Several of the second-hand trolleybuses bought in the 1950's and early 1960's were for spares only, and were never intended to enter service. These included chassis from Darlington and Mexborough. However some others were earmarked for service and allocated fleet numbers (as well as appearing in official fleet lists) but in the end never saw service on Bradford's roads.

T404 (GHN 404) – ex Darlington single decker kept in working order ready to enter service. It never did so and was scrapped.

820-821 (FTE 400-401) ex Ashton Corporation Karrier W with utility Roe bodies. Planned to be rebodied with East Lancs 66 seat bodies. Vehicles subsequently scrapped.

822-825/827 (AEE 22-25/7) ex Grimsby/Cleethorpes Karrier W with Roe bodies. Planned to be rebodied with East Lancs 66 bodies . Vehicles subsequently scrapped.

The new bodies intended for the Ashton and Grimsby/Cleethorpes vehicles were built onto the Mexborough chassis which became 841 – 847.

CHILDREN'S FARES

Children over 5 and under 15 years of age—Half ordinary fare.
Fractions of 1d. count as 1d.

A child under 5 years of age accompanied by a fare paying passenger will be conveyed free, provided it does not occupy a seat required by a fare paying passenger, but no more than one child may accompany such passenger without charge; each additional child will be charged Children's Fares.

Scholars up to $15\frac{1}{2}$ years of age, travelling on school duties or activities, may travel at Children's Fares.

Scholars between $15\frac{1}{2}$ and 18 years may travel on school duties or activities at Children's Fares on production of a Scholar's Pass during school term only, and between the hours of:—

Weekdays:	7.30 a.m. — 5.30 p.m.
Saturdays:	7.30 a.m. — 1.0 p.m.

FINALE

118.   The reinstatement of part-trolleybus operation on 7th March 1972 using 11 vehicles (following a strike in the coal industry early in 1972), allowed plans for the closure of the system to be set for the last week-end in March. The final normal service trolleybuses operated on the night of Friday 24th March. 706 operated the last Duckworth Lane journey, leaving Sunbridge Road at 10.52 pm. The final journey of all was the 10.57pm departure from Thornton Road to Thornton, operated by 843. Both journeys were besieged by enthusiasts and, because the Transport Department would not allow any trolleybus duplicates to these journeys, many were left disappointed. This photograph shows 843 loading outside the Gaumont cinema before departure to Thornton. In its previous life as a single decker at Mexborough, it had been that system's last trolleybus almost exactly eleven years earlier. (A.D.Packer/J.Copland)

119.   On the following Saturday and Sunday morning, pre-bookable tours were operated at £1 per head. The tour started in Thornton Road and proceeded via Thornton, Squire Lane, Duckworth Lane Sunbridge Road and Leeds Road, to Thornbury terminus, returning via Leeds Road to the city centre. On the final tour, departing at 11.30 am on Sunday 26th March, eight trolleybuses were required, the last of which, and therefore the last trolleybus to carry the public, was Mexborough 845. Three stops were allowed for photographic purposes, these being at Bell Dean Road, Toller Lane and Evelyn Avenue (Thornbury). This is the scene on the Saturday afternoon tour at the photographic stop on Toller Lane, with the participants almost stopping the traffic. The tour vehicles were Karriers 712 and 706. (J.S.King)

120.   Bradford's (and Britain's) last trolleybus journey commenced from the City Hall at 3pm on Sunday 26th March. Mexborough 844 was decorated with suitable lettering and left the city centre carrying the Lord Mayor and invited guests. The occasion was given added poignancy by the playing of 'Auld Lang Syne' on the City Hall carillon as the vehicle departed. The vehicle was given a police escort and followed by a tower wagon. The route was the same as for the tours except that on reaching Thornbury depot, 844 ran directly down the approach road into the works, where valedictory speeches were made and the power ceremoniously turned off. 844 can be seen being greeted by the tremendous crowds that awaited it at Thornbury as it prepares to turn right from Leeds Road to travel into the works. (Telegraph and Argus)

Extract from 'Final Trolleybus Closure – Instructions to Staff'

VANDALISM

Unfortunately in other parts of the country where similar ceremonies have been held there has been a considerable amount of stripping of vehicles for souvenirs, light bulbs, etc. and conductors should be on their guard against this happening and deal politely but firmly with it should it arise, summoning police assistance if necessary.

OPERATION OF FOREIGN VEHICLES

We are led to believe that it is the intention of certain enthusiasts' societies to tow preserved vehicles into Bradford and operate them on our wiring and Inspectors and staff are asked to keep their eyes open and report anything suspicious to the police. All Inspectors should obtain a list of our licensed trolleybuses from the Chief Inspector.

VISITORS TO BRADFORD

From the bookings already received it is quite clear that several thousand people from all over the country will be in Bradford to take part in these celebrations and I would ask all staff to ensure that their appearance and conduct is such as to reflect credit on the Undertaking we work for.   E. Deakin
                                                              General Manager
                                                              23rd March 1972

Middleton Press

Easebourne Lane, Midhurst, W Sussex. GU29 9AZ Tel: 01730 813169 Fax: 01730 812601
Email: sales@middletonpress.co.uk   www.middletonpress.co.uk
If books are not available from your local transport stockist, order direct post free UK.

BRANCH LINES
Branch Line to Allhallows
Branch Line to Alton
Branch Lines around Ascot
Branch Line to Ashburton
Branch Lines around Bodmin
Branch Line to Bude
Branch Lines around Canterbury
Branch Line to Chard & Yeovil
Branch Line to Cheddar
Branch Line around Cromer
Branch Line to the Derwent Valley
Branch Lines to East Grinstead
Branch Lines of East London
Branch Lines to Effingham Junction
Branch Lines around Exmouth
Branch Lines to Falmouth, Helston & St. Ives
Branch Line to Fairford
Branch Lines to Felixstowe & Aldeburgh
Branch Line around Gosport
Branch Line to Hayling
Branch Lines to Henley, Windsor & Marlow
Branch Line to Hawkhurst
Branch Line to Horsham
Branch Lines around Huntingdon
Branch Line to Ilfracombe
Branch Line to Kingsbridge
Branch Line to Kingswear
Branch Line to Lambourn
Branch Lines to Launceston & Princetown
Branch Lines to Longmoor
Branch Line to Looe
Branch Line to Lyme Regis
Branch Line to Lynton
Branch Lines around March
Branch Lines around Midhurst
Branch Line to Minehead
Branch Line to Moretonhampstead
Branch Lines to Newport (IOW)
Branch Lines to Newquay
Branch Lines around North Woolwich
Branch Line to Padstow
Branch Lines to Princes Risborough
Branch Lines to Seaton and Sidmouth
Branch Lines around Sheerness
Branch Line to Shrewsbury
Branch Line to Tenterden
Branch Lines around Tiverton
Branch Lines to Torrington
Branch Lines to Tunbridge Wells
Branch Line to Upwell
Branch Lines of West London
Branch Lines of West Wiltshire
Branch Lines around Weymouth
Branch Lines around Wimborne
Branch Lines around Wisbech

NARROW GAUGE
Austrian Narrow Gauge
Branch Line to Lynton
Branch Lines around Portmadoc 1923-46
Branch Lines around Porthmadog 1954-94
Branch Line to Southwold
Douglas to Port Erin
Douglas to Peel
Kent Narrow Gauge
Northern France Narrow Gauge
Romneyrail
Southern France Narrow Gauge
Sussex Narrow Gauge
Surrey Narrow Gauge
Swiss Narrow Gauge

Two-Foot Gauge Survivors
Vivarais Narrow Gauge

SOUTH COAST RAILWAYS
Ashford to Dover
Bournemouth to Weymouth
Brighton to Worthing
Dover to Ramsgate
Eastbourne to Hastings
Hastings to Ashford
Portsmouth to Southampton
Ryde to Ventnor
Southampton to Bournemouth

SOUTHERN MAIN LINES
Basingstoke to Salisbury
Crawley to Littlehampton
Dartford to Sittingbourne
East Croydon to Three Bridges
Epsom to Horsham
Exeter to Barnstaple
Exeter to Tavistock
London Bridge to East Croydon
Orpington to Tonbridge
Tonbridge to Hastings
Salisbury to Yeovil
Sittingbourne to Ramsgate
Swanley to Ashford
Tavistock to Plymouth
Three Bridges to Brighton
Victoria to Bromley South
Victoria to East Croydon
Waterloo to Windsor
Waterloo to Woking
Woking to Portsmouth
Woking to Southampton
Yeovil to Exeter

EASTERN MAIN LINES
Barking to Southend
Ely to Kings Lynn
Ely to Norwich
Fenchurch Street to Barking
Hitchin to Peterborough
Ilford to Shenfield
Ipswich to Saxmundham
Liverpool Street to Ilford
Saxmundham to Yarmouth
Tilbury Loop

WESTERN MAIN LINES
Bristol to Taunton
Didcot to Banbury
Didcot to Swindon
Ealing to Slough
Exeter to Newton Abbot
Newton Abbot to Plymouth
Newbury to Westbury
Oxford to Moreton-in-Marsh
Paddington to Ealing
Paddington to Princes Risborough
Plymouth to St. Austell
Princes Risborough to Banbury
Reading to Didcot
Slough to Newbury
St. Austell to Penzance
Swindon to Bristol
Taunton to Exeter
Westbury to Taunton

MIDLAND MAIN LINES
St. Albans to Bedford
Euston to Harrow & Wealdstone

Harrow to Watford
St. Pancras to St. Albans

COUNTRY RAILWAY ROUTES
Abergavenny to Merthyr
Andover to Southampton
Bath to Evercreech Junction
Bath Green Park to Bristol
Bournemouth to Evercreech Junction
Brecon to Newport
Burnham to Evercreech Junction
Cheltenham to Andover
Croydon to East Grinstead
Didcot to Winchester
East Kent Light Railway
Frome to Bristol
Guildford to Redhill
Reading to Basingstoke
Reading to Guildford
Redhill to Ashford
Salisbury to Westbury
Stratford upon Avon to Cheltenham
Strood to Paddock Wood
Taunton to Barnstaple
Wenford Bridge to Fowey
Westbury to Bath
Woking to Alton
Yeovil to Dorchester

GREAT RAILWAY ERAS
Ashford from Steam to Eurostar
Clapham Junction 50 years of change
Festiniog in the Fifties
Festiniog in the Sixties
Festiniog 50 years of enterprise
Isle of Wight Lines 50 years of change
Railways to Victory 1944-46
Return to Blaenau 1970-82
SECR Centenary album
Talyllyn 50 years of change
Wareham to Swanage 50 years of change
Yeovil 50 years of change

LONDON SUBURBAN RAILWAYS
Caterham and Tattenham Corner
Charing Cross to Dartford
Clapham Jn. to Beckenham Jn.
Crystal Palace (HL) & Catford Loop
East London Line
Finsbury Park to Alexandra Palace
Holborn Viaduct to Lewisham
Kingston and Hounslow Loops
Lewisham to Dartford
Liverpool Street to Chingford
London Bridge to Addiscombe
Mitcham Junction Lines
North London Line
South London Line
West Croydon to Epsom
West London Line
Willesden Junction to Richmond
Wimbledon to Beckenham
Wimbledon to Epsom

STEAMING THROUGH
Steaming through Cornwall
Steaming through the Isle of Wight
Steaming through Kent
Steaming through West Hants

TRAMWAY CLASSICS
Aldgate & Stepney Tramways
Barnet & Finchley Tramways

Bath Tramways
Brighton's Tramways
Bristol's Tramways
Burton & Ashby Tramways
Camberwell & W.Norwood Tramways
Clapham & Streatham Tramways
Croydon's Tramways
Dover's Tramways
East Ham & West Ham Tramways
Edgware and Willesden Tramways
Eltham & Woolwich Tramways
Embankment & Waterloo Tramways
Exeter & Taunton Tramways
Fulwell - Home to Trams, Trolleys and Buses
Great Yarmouth Tramways
Greenwich & Dartford Tramways
Hammersmith & Hounslow Tramways
Hampstead & Highgate Tramways
Hastings Tramways
Holborn & Finsbury Tramways
Ilford & Barking Tramways
Kingston & Wimbledon Tramways
Lewisham & Catford Tramways
Liverpool Tramways 1. Eastern Routes
Liverpool Tramways 2. Southern Routes
Liverpool Tramways 3. Northern Routes
Maidstone & Chatham Tramways
Margate to Ramsgate
North Kent Tramways
Norwich Tramways
Reading Tramways
Seaton & Eastbourne Tramways
Shepherds Bush & Uxbridge Tramways
Southend-on-sea Tramways
South London Line Tramways 1903-33
Southwark & Deptford Tramways
Stamford Hill Tramways
Twickenham & Kingston Tramways
Victoria & Lambeth Tramways
Waltham Cross & Edmonton Tramways
Walthamstow & Leyton Tramways
Wandsworth & Battersea Tramways

TROLLEYBUS CLASSICS
Bradford Trolleybuses
Croydon Trolleybuses
Derby Trolleybuses
Hastings Trolleybuses
Huddersfield Trolleybuses
Maidstone Trolleybuses
Portsmouth Trolleybuses
Reading Trolleybuses

WATERWAY ALBUMS
Kent and East Sussex Waterways
London to Portsmouth Waterway
West Sussex Waterways

MILITARY BOOKS
Battle over Portsmouth
Battle over Sussex 1940
Blitz over Sussex 1941-42
Bombers over Sussex 1943-45
Bognor at War
Military Defence of West Sussex
Military Signals from the South Coast
Secret Sussex Resistance
Surrey Home Guard

OTHER RAILWAY BOOKS
Index to all Middleton Press stations
Industrial Railways of the South-East
South Eastern & Chatham Railways
London Chatham & Dover Railway
London Termini - Past and Proposed
War on the Line (SR 1939-45)